THE AUSTRALIAN
Women's Weekly

cookingclass

thai

step-by-step to perfect results

contents

Thai food has captivated the Western palate and who doesn't remember their first experience of that distinctive Thai genius for combining sweet and sour, sharp and fresh flavours: lime, chilli, coriander, galangal, basil and coconut? While sophisticated in taste, Thai cuisine is simple to prepare. It employs fresh ingredients and quick and easy cooking techniques, making it ideal for home preparation. Thai ingredients are now readily available in large supermarkets and specialist Asian food shops.

Pamela Clark

Food Director

thai essential ingredients

With just a few basic but distinctive ingredients, you'll find that your Thai meals will taste authentic every time.

lemon grass

A vital ingredient in Thai cooking, fresh lemon grass is available from Asian food stores and most supermarkets. The top green leaves are discarded and only the bulbous lower stem is used. When preparing lemon grass, the tough outer layers should be peeled away leaving the pale inner portion of the lower stem. Trimmed stalks can be well-wrapped and refrigerated or frozen.

kaffir lime leaves and limes

The kaffir lime, both leaves and fruit, imparts a tangy citrus flavour to many Thai dishes. While the dried leaves are readily available, the fresh ones are preferable and it is often possible to find them in larger supermarkets. Where fresh leaves are specified, such as in a salad, you can substitute fresh young lemon or lime leaves, although dried leaves are perfectly acceptable in cooked food. The knobbly-skinned kaffir lime fruit can be difficult to find and the readily available Tahitian lime is a good substitute. Both fruit and leaves of the kaffir lime can be frozen.

fish sauce

Known in Thailand as *nam pla*, fish sauce is made from the clear brown liquid drained from barrels of fermented anchovies. Its pungent fishy aroma can take a little getting used to at first, but the salty piquancy it adds makes it an essential ingredient for an authentic Thai taste.

coconut

Coconut features in a great deal of Thai cooking. Both coconut cream and coconut milk are readily available in cans, although you can also make milk by combining 2 cups desiccated coconut with 2 1/2 cups hot water. Allow to cool, blend or process for 20 seconds, then strain, pressing out all liquid. Coconut milk powder is also available from supermarkets. When reconstituted, it is a good substitute for coconut milk but is not as rich as coconut cream.

fresh coriander leaves and roots

A strongly flavoured herb also known as cilantro, fresh coriander imparts a distinctive flavour to Thai food. All parts of the plant are used, including the roots which are an essential ingredient in curry pastes. (The dried seeds, whole or ground, of the coriander plant are never a substitute for fresh leaves.) Store coriander in the refrigerator.

thai basil

Fresh basil is an indispensable ingredient in Thai cooking and a number of different types of basil are used. While Thais mainly use *horapa*, similar to our common sweet basil, and a smaller-leafed, more pungent variety called *kaprao* or holy basil, we have used fresh sweet basil in all the recipes in this book where basil is specified.

jasmine rice

Thai meals are always based on rice, usually jasmine rice, a long-grained variety named for its delicately perfumed flavour. It is cooked, without salt, by the absorption method and served with a variety of other dishes and soups.

absorption method

Rinse 2 cups jasmine rice in strainer under cold water until water runs clear. Combine 3 1/2 cups water and rice in heavy-base saucepan; bring to a boil, stirring, reduce heat to as low as possible. Cover tightly and cook for 12 minutes. Do not remove lid during cooking. Remove pan from heat; stand, covered, 10 minutes. Fluff with a fork. Serves 4.

1 *Rinse uncooked rice until water runs clear.*

2 *Combine rice and water in saucepan, cover; bring to a boil.*

3 *Fluff cooked rice with a fork so that it doesn't "clump" while standing.*

entrees

Serving entrees just before the main course, as in Western meals, is virtually unknown in Thai households. Instead, entrees are sometimes served to guests before they sit down at the dinner table. Snacks are also served throughout the day, and at parties and celebrations. Several of our entrees can easily be modified into main courses using a dash of flexibility and imagination.

mixed satay

PREPARATION TIME 50 MINUTES (plus refrigerating time) • COOKING TIME 35 MINUTES (plus cooling time)

250g chicken breast fillets, sliced
250g piece beef eye fillet, sliced
250g pork fillets, sliced
2 cloves garlic, crushed
1/2 teaspoon ground coriander
1/4 teaspoon ground cumin
1/2 teaspoon curry powder
2 tablespoons oil
1 tablespoon brown sugar
1 tablespoon fish sauce
1/4 teaspoon sambal oelek

SATAY SAUCE
1 cup (150g) peanuts
1 tablespoon oil
1 medium brown onion (150g), finely chopped
2 cloves garlic, crushed
2 medium fresh red chillies, finely chopped
1 tablespoon finely chopped fresh lemon grass
1/2 teaspoon curry powder
1/4 teaspoon ground cumin

1/4 teaspoon chopped fresh coriander root
1 cup (250ml) coconut milk
2 tablespoons brown sugar
2 teaspoons tamarind sauce
2 teaspoons lime juice

SWEET AND SOUR SAUCE
1/4 cup (60ml) white vinegar
1/2 cup (110g) sugar
1 1/2 tablespoons water
1/2 small carrot (35g), finely chopped
1/4 small green cucumber (65g), seeded, chopped

1 Thread chicken, beef and pork onto skewers; place in shallow dish. Combine garlic, coriander, cumin, curry powder, oil, sugar, sauce and sambal oelek in bowl; pour over skewers. Cover, refrigerate skewers for at least 1 hour.

2 Grill skewers until tender, turning often; serve with sauces.

satay sauce Blend or process peanuts until crushed. Heat oil in wok, add onion, garlic, chillies, lemon grass, curry powder, cumin and coriander root. Cook, stirring, until onion is soft. Add peanuts and remaining ingredients, stir until hot.

sweet and sour sauce Combine vinegar, sugar and water in pan, stir until sugar is dissolved, bring to boil. Boil, uncovered, for 3 minutes. Pour syrup over carrot and cucumber in serving bowl; cool.

MAKES 30

store Satay skewers can be prepared a day ahead; sauces made 6 hours ahead. Store satay skewers, covered, in refrigerator; sauces, covered, at room temperature. Uncooked satay skewers suitable to freeze.
per skewer chicken 1.9g fat; 180kJ; **beef** 2.9g fat; 207kJ;
pork 3.4g fat; 227kJ
sauce, per tablespoon satay 5g fat; 242kJ;
sweet and sour 0.02g fat; 371kJ

Pouring marinade over skewers

peanut curry with eggs

PREPARATION TIME 10 MINUTES • COOKING TIME 10 MINUTES

2 tablespoons red curry paste
1/2 teaspoon canned drained
  green peppercorns
1/4 teaspoon ground cardamom
2 teaspoons paprika
21/2 cups (625ml)
  coconut milk
1/2 teaspoon palm sugar
2 tablespoons fish sauce
250g frozen peas, thawed
8 hard-boiled eggs, halved
1/2 cup (75g) coarsely
  chopped peanuts

1 Combine paste, peppercorns and
   spices in pan. Add 1/2 cup of the
   coconut milk to the curry paste
   mixture, cook 1 minute or until
   fragrant.

2 Combine remaining coconut milk,
   sugar, sauce, peas and curry
   mixture in pan, stir until heated
   through; pour curry around eggs,
   sprinkle with peanuts.

SERVES 6

store Curry paste mixture can
be prepared a week ahead. Store,
covered, in refrigerator.
per serving 39.9g fat; 1888kJ

Adding coconut milk to curry paste mixture

Combining remaining ingredients

Combining ingredients in a bowl

Dropping corn mixture into hot oil

corn and chicken fritters

PREPARATION TIME 15 MINUTES • COOKING TIME 20 MINUTES

2 eggs, lightly beaten
2 x 440g cans corn kernels,
  drained
2 tablespoons cornflour
250g chicken breast fillets,
  chopped
2 teaspoons chopped
  fresh coriander leaves
1 teaspoon sugar
1 tablespoon light soy sauce
2 tablespoons oil

1 Combine eggs, corn, cornflour, chicken, coriander, sugar and sauce in bowl; mix well.

2 Heat oil in pan, drop level tablespoons of corn mixture into pan, cook on both sides until well browned and cooked; drain on absorbent paper.

MAKES ABOUT 40

store Batter can be prepared 3 hours ahead. Store covered, in refrigerator.
per fritter 1.5g fat; 157kJ

beef and prawn pouches

PREPARATION TIME 35 MINUTES • COOKING TIME 35 MINUTES (plus cooling time)

2 tablespoons oil
1 clove garlic, crushed
1 small brown onion (80g),
    finely chopped
2 teaspoons chopped fresh ginger
80g minced beef
60g cooked small prawns, shelled
1 small carrot (70g), grated
2 green onions, chopped
1 tablespoon chopped fresh
    basil leaves
1 tablespoon sugar
250g packet gow gee wrappers
1 egg, lightly beaten
oil for deep-frying
1 medium fresh red chilli, sliced

SWEET CHILLI SAUCE
1/2 cup (125ml) water
1/4 cup (60ml) white vinegar
1 teaspoon hoisin sauce
1 small fresh red chilli, chopped
1/2 cup (100g) brown sugar,
    firmly packed

1 Heat oil in pan, cook garlic, stirring, until lightly browned.
   Add brown onion and ginger, cook, stirring, 1 minute. Add mince, cook,
   stirring, until mince is well browned. Stir in prawns, carrot and green
   onion, cook 1 minute; cool. Stir in basil and sugar.

2 Brush gow gee wrappers with egg, top with level teaspoons of
   mince mixture. Pull up edges of wrapper around mixture,
   pinch together to seal.

3 Deep-fry pouches in hot oil, in batches, until well browned; drain on
   absorbent paper. Serve hot pouches with hot sweet chilli sauce; top with
   sliced chilli.

sweet chilli sauce Combine all ingredients in pan, stir over heat until
sugar is dissolved. Bring to boil, simmer, uncovered, for about 5 minutes
or until slightly thickened.

MAKES 30

store Pouches can be prepared 3 hours ahead. Store, covered, in refrigerator.
Uncooked pouches suitable to freeze. Sweet chilli sauce can be prepared
2 days ahead. Store, covered, in refrigerator.
per pouch 4.2g fat; 282kJ

Preparing mince mixture

Enclosing mixture in gow gee wrappers

Deep-frying pouches

spring rolls with chilli and peanut sauce

PREPARATION TIME 40 MINUTES (plus standing time) • COOKING TIME 35 MINUTES (plus cooling time)

50g rice vermicelli
250g lean pork
1 tablespoon oil
1 clove garlic, crushed
1 teaspoon chopped fresh
  red chillies
2 green onions, chopped
1 medium carrot (120g), grated
1 tablespoon chopped fresh
  coriander root
1 tablespoon chopped fresh
  coriander leaves
1 teaspoon fish sauce
100g cooked prawns,
  shelled, chopped
30 spring roll pastry sheets
1 tablespoon cornflour
2 tablespoons water
oil for deep-frying

CHILLI AND PEANUT SAUCE
1/4 cup (60ml) white vinegar
2 tablespoons sugar
1/2 small green cucumber (65g),
  peeled, seeded, chopped
1/4 teaspoon chopped fresh
  red chilli
1 tablespoon chopped peanuts

1 Cover vermicelli with warm water in bowl, stand 10 minutes; drain well. Chop vermicelli.

2 Process pork until finely minced. Heat oil in pan, cook pork, garlic and chillies, stirring, until pork is browned. Add onions, carrot, coriander root and leaves, sauce, prawns and vermicelli. Cook, stirring, until hot; cool.

3 Place level tablespoons of mixture on a corner of each pastry sheet, brush edges with blended cornflour and water. Fold left and right corners inwards, then bottom corner inwards. Roll pastry sheet to enclose filling.

4 Deep-fry rolls in hot oil until well browned; drain on absorbent paper. Serve hot spring rolls with chilli and peanut sauce.

chilli and peanut sauce Combine vinegar and sugar in pan, stir over heat until sugar is dissolved. Bring to boil, simmer, uncovered, for about 4 minutes or until syrup just begins to colour. Remove syrup from heat, transfer to bowl; cool slightly. Stir in remaining ingredients.

MAKES 30

store Rolls can be prepared 3 hours ahead. Store, covered, in refrigerator.
per spring roll 2.6g fat; 294kJ

Standing vermicelli in warm water

Rolling mixture in spring roll sheets

Deep-frying spring rolls

red curry fish cakes

PREPARATION TIME 45 MINUTES • COOKING TIME 15 MINUTES

1kg redfish fillets
1 egg
2 teaspoons chopped fresh
    coriander leaves
2 teaspoons sugar
100g green beans, thinly sliced
oil for deep-frying

RED CURRY PASTE
1 small red onion (100g), chopped
3 cloves garlic, crushed
2 tablespoons chopped fresh
    lemon grass
3 teaspoons chopped fresh
    coriander root
2 teaspoons dried chilli flakes
1 teaspoon galangal powder
1 teaspoon grated lime rind
1/2 teaspoon shrimp paste
1 dried kaffir lime leaf
3 teaspoons paprika
1/2 teaspoon ground turmeric
1/2 teaspoon cumin seeds
3 teaspoons oil

1   Blend or process fish, egg, coriander, sugar and 1/3 cup of red curry paste until well combined and smooth. Reserve remaining red curry paste for another use.

2   Combine fish mixture and beans in bowl; mix well.

3   Roll 2 level tablespoons of mixture into a ball, flatten slightly; repeat with remaining mixture.

4   Deep-fry fish cakes in hot oil until well browned and cooked; drain on absorbent paper.

red curry paste   Blend or process all ingredients until smooth.

MAKES 25

store   Fish cakes can be prepared a day ahead; red curry paste can be made a week ahead. Store, covered, in refrigerator. Uncooked fish cakes suitable to freeze.
per fish cake   7g fat; 424kJ

Shaping fish cake mixture

Deep-frying fish cakes

Shaping mixture over egg white halves

Dipping egg halves in batter

crispy eggs with pork and prawn

PREPARATION TIME 30 MINUTES (plus refrigerating and standing Time) • COOKING TIME 25 MINUTES

8 hard-boiled eggs
200g cooked prawns, shelled,
   finely chopped
200g minced pork
2 tablespoons coconut cream
2 tablespoons chopped fresh
   coriander leaves
1 tablespoon fish sauce
oil for deep-frying

BATTER
1/2 cup (75g) plain flour
1/2 cup (75g) self-raising flour
1 teaspoon sugar
2 tablespoons oil
1 cup (250ml) water

1 Cut eggs in half, remove yolks. Mash egg yolks in bowl with fork, add prawns, pork, coconut cream, coriander and sauce; mix well. Divide pork mixture into 16 portions. Shape portions over egg white halves to form egg shapes. Cover, refrigerate 1 hour.

2 Dip egg halves into batter, deep-fry in hot oil until browned and cooked through; drain on absorbent paper. Serve hot.

batter Sift flours and sugar into bowl, gradually stir in oil and water, beat to a smooth batter (or blend or process ingredients until smooth). Cover, stand 20 minutes.

MAKES 16

store Eggs can be prepared a day ahead. Store, covered, in refrigerator.
per egg half 14.7g fat; 814.6kJ

soups

Soups are usually served as part of the main Thai meal and can be eaten separately or spooned onto your plate and eaten with rice. Clear hot and sour Thai soups are memorable for their subtle yet bold combination of flavours using lemon grass, lemon juice and chilli. We've also included some richer soups using noodles and coconut milk.

mixed seafood soup

PREPARATION TIME 25 MINUTES • COOKING TIME 1 HOUR (plus cooling time)

250g uncooked king prawns
6 baby octopus (500g)
8 cups (2 litres) water
2 tablespoons oil
1 small brown onion (80g),
  finely chopped
3 teaspoons grated fresh ginger
3 cloves garlic, crushed
1 stem fresh lemon grass,
  finely chopped
pinch saffron powder
1 fresh coriander root,
  finely chopped
1 teaspoon sweet chilli sauce
1 1/2 tablespoons fish sauce
1/3 cup (80ml) lime juice
4 dried kaffir lime leaves
1/2 teaspoon cumin seeds
400ml coconut cream
1 tablespoon raw sugar
160g scallops
250g white fish fillets, chopped
2 tablespoons fresh coriander leaves

1 Shell prawns, reserve heads. Remove heads and beaks from octopus, cut tentacles into pairs.

2 Combine reserved prawn heads with water in pan, slowly bring to boil; simmer, uncovered, for 30 minutes. Cool stock, strain; reserve stock.

3 Heat oil in pan, cook onion, ginger, garlic, lemon grass, saffron, coriander root and sauces, stirring, until onion is soft.

4 Add reserved stock, juice, lime leaves and seeds, bring to boil; simmer, uncovered, for 15 minutes. Stir in coconut cream and sugar, simmer 5 minutes.

5 Stir in seafood; simmer for about 2 minutes or until seafood is tender. Sprinkle with coriander.

SERVES 6

store Can be prepared a day ahead. Store, covered, in refrigerator.
per serving 22g fat; 1377kJ

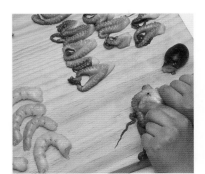

Preparing the seafood

Preparing the stock

Adding the seafood

spicy beef soup

PREPARATION TIME 15 MINUTES (plus standing time) • COOKING TIME 25 MINUTES

**375g beef round steak,
 thinly sliced**
1 tablespoon dry red wine
6 cups (1.5 litres) water
2 beef stock cubes, crumbled
6 green onions, chopped
2 cloves garlic, sliced
3 fresh coriander roots
2 tablespoons dark soy sauce
2 teaspoons brown sugar
**1 small fresh red chilli,
 finely chopped**
**425g can straw mushrooms,
 drained**
1/4 cup (60ml) lime juice
**1 tablespoon chopped fresh
 coriander leaves**

1 Combine steak and wine in bowl;
   cover, stand 15 minutes.

2 Combine water, stock cubes,
   onion, garlic, coriander roots,
   sauce, sugar and half the chilli
   in pan. Bring to boil, simmer,
   uncovered, for 15 minutes. Drain
   mixture, return liquid to pan,
   discard pulp.

3 Bring stock to boil, add steak,
   mushrooms, remaining chilli and
   juice, simmer, uncovered, until
   hot. Stir in coriander leaves.

SERVES 6

store Can be prepared a day
ahead. Store, covered, in
refrigerator.
per serving 3.5g fat; 433kJ

Combining steak and wine in a bowl

Adding straw mushrooms

Stirring in coconut cream

Adding prawns to soup

pumpkin and coconut cream soup

PREPARATION TIME 15 MINUTES • COOKING TIME 30 MINUTES

1 tablespoon oil
1 clove garlic, crushed
4 green onions, chopped
2 small fresh red chillies, chopped
1 tablespoon chopped fresh
**   lemon grass**
1/2 teaspoon shrimp paste
2 cups (500ml) boiling
**   chicken stock**
500g pumpkin, chopped
400ml coconut cream
250g cooked small prawns, shelled
1 tablespoon shredded fresh
**   basil leaves**

1 Heat oil in pan, add garlic, onion, chilli, lemon grass and paste. Cook, stirring, until onion is soft.

2 Add stock, bring to boil. Add pumpkin, simmer, covered, for 10 minutes. Stir in coconut cream, simmer, covered, for 5 minutes or until pumpkin is tender.

3 Add prawns, stir until hot. Serve soup sprinkled with basil.

SERVES 4

store Can be made a day ahead. Store, covered, in refrigerator.
per serving 26.2g fat; 1391kJ

chicken and noodle soup

PREPARATION TIME 15 MINUTES • COOKING TIME 25 MINUTES

400g chicken breast fillets
2 cloves garlic, crushed
3 teaspoons ground cumin
1/2 teaspoon ground turmeric
6 cups (11/2 litres) water
2 teaspoons chicken stock powder
1 tablespoon sugar
1/2 teaspoon shrimp paste
3 teaspoons sambal oelek
1 piece dried galangal
50g rice vermicelli
1 cup (100g) bean sprouts
3 lettuce leaves, shredded
2 tablespoons chopped fresh
  coriander leaves

1 Cut chicken into 2cm slices. Combine garlic, cumin and turmeric in pan, stir over heat for about 1 minute or until fragrant.

2 Add chicken, water, stock powder, sugar, paste, sambal oelek and galangal to pan, stir until combined. Bring to boil; simmer, uncovered, for 10 minutes.

3 Add vermicelli to pan, simmer for 10 minutes.

4 Stir in bean sprouts, lettuce and coriander.

SERVES 6

store Can be prepared a day ahead. Store, covered, in refrigerator.
per serving 3.3g fat; 528kJ

Stirring spices over heat

Adding vermicelli to pan

Adding chopped lettuce to soup

chicken and coconut milk soup (tom kha gai)

PREPARATION TIME 20 MINUTES • COOKING TIME 20 MINUTES

500g chicken breast fillets
5 cups (1.25 litres)
   coconut milk
5 dried kaffir lime leaves
4 pieces dried galangal
1 stem fresh lemon
   grass, sliced
2 tablespoons lemon juice
1/2 teaspoon sugar
2 tablespoons fish sauce
2 teaspoons chopped fresh
   red chillies
5 green onions, shredded

1 Cut chicken into 1cm strips.

2 Combine coconut milk, leaves,
  galangal and lemon grass in
  pan, bring to boil. Add chicken;
  simmer, uncovered, until chicken
  is tender.

3 Stir in juice, sugar, sauce, chilli
  and onion. Bring to boil, simmer,
  uncovered, for 3 minutes.

SERVES 4

store Best made just before
serving.
per serving 75.5g fat; 3513kJ

Cutting chicken into strips

Adding chilli to pan

Shelling prawns leaving tails intact

Making fish stock

hot and sour prawn soup (tom yum goong)

PREPARATION TIME 25 MINUTES • COOKING TIME 40 MINUTES (plus refrigerating time)

500g uncooked prawns
2 small fresh red chillies, chopped
1 tablespoon sliced fresh lemon grass
1 teaspoon grated fresh ginger
2 teaspoons fish sauce
2 teaspoons light soy sauce
1 tablespoon lime juice
2 teaspoons sugar
4 green onions, chopped
425g can whole straw mushrooms, rinsed, drained

FISH STOCK
500g white fish bones
10 cups (2.5 litres) water
2 stems fresh lemon grass, chopped
1 small fresh red chilli, halved
4 dried kaffir lime leaves
3 pieces dried galangal

1 Shell prawns leaving tails intact. Measure 6 cups of stock into pan, leaving sediment in pan.

2 Add prawns, chilli, lemon grass, ginger, sauces, juice, sugar, onion and mushrooms. Bring to boil, simmer, uncovered, until prawns are tender.

fish stock Combine all ingredients in pan, bring to boil; simmer, covered, for 20 minutes. Strain stock through fine strainer; cover, refrigerate overnight.

SERVES 4

store Stock best made a day ahead. Store, covered, in refrigerator. Stock suitable to freeze.
per serving 1g fat; 369kJ

salads

Vegetables are generally eaten raw, dipped in sauces, served over a bed of lettuce and garnished with coriander leaves. They are also stir-fried or lightly steamed, and sometimes small amounts of fish, minced meat or chicken are added as a flavour contrast. Our recipes can be served as accompaniments to a main meal or simply as a light meal.

tofu and egg salad

PREPARATION TIME 25 MINUTES (plus standing time) • COOKING TIME 15 MINUTES (plus cooling time)

**2 teaspoons chopped fresh
  coriander root**
1 clove garlic, crushed
1 tablespoon grated fresh ginger
2 tablespoons brown sugar
2 tablespoons dark soy sauce
1 teaspoon five-spice powder
2 teaspoons oil
1/4 cup (60ml) water
6 radishes (200g)
375g tofu, drained, cubed
**1 tablespoon chopped fresh
  coriander leaves**
**1 small fresh red chilli,
  finely chopped**
1 hard-boiled egg, chopped

1 Blend coriander root, garlic, ginger, sugar, sauce and five-spice powder until well combined.

2 Heat oil in pan, cook blended mixture, stirring, for about 2 minutes or until fragrant. Stir in water; cool to room temperature.

3 Cut radishes into thin strips. Combine tofu and radish in bowl, pour over blended mixture; cover, stand for 2 hours, stirring occasionally.

4 Drain tofu mixture, combine with coriander leaves, chilli and egg.

SERVES 4

store Can be prepared 6 hours ahead. Store, covered, in refrigerator.
per serving 9.6g fat; 835kJ

Adding water to spice mixture

Pouring spice mixture over tofu and radish

Adding coriander and chilli

beans with ginger and coconut milk

PREPARATION TIME 15 MINUTES • COOKING TIME 10 MINUTES

500g green beans
1 tablespoon oil
2 stems fresh lemon grass,
  finely chopped
2 tablespoons grated
  fresh ginger
1 small fresh red
  chilli, chopped
1 cup (250ml) coconut milk
4 cups (350g) shredded
  cabbage

1 Cut beans into 5cm lengths.
  Heat oil in wok, cook lemon
  grass, ginger and chilli until
  oil begins to bubble.

2 Stir in coconut milk and beans,
  bring to boil; simmer, uncovered,
  for about 3 minutes or until
  beans are just tender. Serve
  bean mixture over cabbage.

SERVES 6

store Best made close
to serving.
per serving 13.1g fat; 620kJ

Adding spices to hot oil

Stirring in coconut milk

Combining dressing in bowl

Pouring dressing over fruit and nuts

fruit salad with savoury coconut dressing

PREPARATION TIME 20 MINUTES (plus refrigerating time)

1 medium apple (150g)
1 medium banana (200g)
¹/₂ medium papaw (500g)
1 cup (250ml) coconut milk
1 small fresh red chilli, chopped
**1 tablespoon chopped fresh
   coriander leaves**
2 tablespoons lime juice
1 tablespoon fish sauce
¹/₄ cup (35g) peanuts
6 cos lettuce leaves

1 Cut apple in half, remove core, cut into thin slices; slice banana; chop papaw. Combine coconut milk, chilli, coriander, juice and sauce in bowl.

2 Combine fruit and peanuts in bowl with coconut milk dressing, mix well; cover, refrigerate 1 hour before serving. Serve over lettuce.

SERVES 4

store Best made 1 hour ahead. Store, covered, in refrigerator.
per serving 19g fat; 1159kJ

stir-fried sweet and sour vegetables

PREPARATION TIME 20 MINUTES • COOKING TIME 10 MINUTES

2 cloves garlic
2 small fresh red chillies
500g fresh asparagus
2 Lebanese cucumbers (260g)
1 tablespoon oil
100g snow peas
250g broccoli flowerets
1 medium green capsicum
   (200g), chopped
2 tablespoons fish sauce
1¹/₂ tablespoons white vinegar
1 tablespoon sugar

1 Cut garlic and chillies into long, thin strips. Cut asparagus into 5cm lengths; cut cucumbers in half lengthways, remove seeds, then slice thickly.

2 Heat oil in wok, stir-fry garlic and chillies until lightly browned; remove from wok. Leave oil in wok.

3 Reheat wok, add vegetables, stir-fry until vegetables are just tender.

4 Add combined sauce, vinegar and sugar, stir-fry 1 minute. Serve vegetables sprinkled with garlic and chillies.

SERVES 6

store Best made close to serving.
per serving 3.5g fat; 322kJ

Preparing vegetables

Stir-frying garlic and chilli

Adding combined sauce, vinegar and sugar

spicy tofu salad

PREPARATION TIME 20 MINUTES (plus refrigerating time)

750g tofu, drained
1 small red onion (100g)
1 medium carrot (120g)
1 medium green capsicum (200g)
2 tablespoons peanuts, chopped

DRESSING
2 small fresh red chillies, finely chopped
1/4 cup (60ml) lime juice
2 tablespoons brown sugar
1 tablespoon fish sauce
1 stem fresh lemon grass, thinly sliced

1 Cut tofu into 1cm cubes. Cut onion in half, cut into thin slices.
   Cut carrot and capsicum into thin strips.

2 Combine tofu, onion, carrot, capsicum and dressing in bowl; mix well.
   Cover, refrigerate 3 hours. Serve salad sprinkled with peanuts.

   dressing Combine chilli, juice, sugar, sauce and lemon grass in jar;
   shake well.

SERVES 6

store Salad can be made 3 hours ahead. Store, covered, in refrigerator.
per serving 8.2g fat; 807kJ

Cutting tofu into cubes

Combining tofu and dressing

sweet and sour tofu

PREPARATION TIME 15 MINUTES • COOKING TIME 20 MINUTES

375g tofu, drained
1/4 cup (60ml) oil
1 clove garlic, sliced
200g green beans, sliced
1 medium white onion
   (150g), sliced
1 medium carrot (120g), sliced
200g broccoli, chopped
1 stick celery, sliced
2 green onions, chopped
1 tablespoon tamarind sauce
1 tablespoon fish sauce
2 tablespoons oyster sauce
1 tablespoon light soy sauce
1 tablespoon sweet chilli sauce
1 tablespoon tomato paste
2 tablespoons sugar
1 tablespoon white vinegar
1/4 teaspoon ground star anise
1 teaspoon cornflour
1 cup (250ml) water

1 Cut tofu into 1.5cm cubes.

2 Heat oil in wok, cook garlic 30 seconds, remove and discard garlic. Add tofu to wok in batches, stir-fry gently until lightly browned; remove from wok.

3 Add beans, white onion and carrot, stir-fry until vegetables are almost tender. Add broccoli, celery and green onion, sauces, paste, sugar, vinegar and spice; stir-fry 2 minutes. Stir in tofu with blended cornflour and water; stir-fry gently until sauce boils and thickens slightly.

SERVES 6

store Best made close to serving.
per serving 13g fat; 965kJ

Cutting tofu into cubes

Adding blended cornflour and water

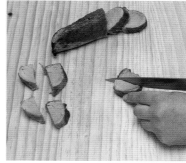
Cutting pork

Adding fish sauce

water chestnut salad with fillet of pork

PREPARATION TIME 20 MINUTES • COOKING TIME 15 MINUTES (plus cooling time)

1 tablespoon oil
250g pork fillet
8 green onions
3 cloves garlic, sliced
1 tablespoon fish sauce
2 tablespoons lemon juice
3 teaspoons sugar
**8 medium cooked prawns
    (165g), shelled**
50g crab meat, flaked
230g can water chestnuts, drained
**1 tablespoon chopped fresh
    coriander leaves**

1 Heat oil in pan, cook pork, turning frequently, until well browned and tender. Remove pork from pan, drain, cool. Cut into 1cm slices, then cut into halves.

2 Cut onions into 6cm strips. Reheat pan, stir-fry garlic and onion for 1 minute; add sauce, juice and sugar, stir-fry until hot; cool.

3 Combine pork, onion mixture, prawns, crab and water chestnuts in bowl, sprinkle with coriander.

SERVES 4

store Pork can be prepared a day ahead; onion mixture several hours ahead. Store, covered, in refrigerator.
per serving 6.1g fat; 732kJ

mixed vegetables with mushrooms

PREPARATION TIME 25 MINUTES • COOKING TIME 15 MINUTES

1 small zucchini (90g)
1 medium carrot (120g)
2 tablespoons oil
3 small fresh red chillies,
  finely chopped
1 stem fresh lemon grass,
  finely chopped
¹/₂ cup (125ml) coconut milk
1 dried kaffir lime leaf
100g green beans, sliced
1 small red capsicum
  (150g), sliced
150g broccoli, chopped
425g can straw mushrooms,
  drained
1 tablespoon chopped fresh
  basil leaves
500g Chinese broccoli, shredded

1 Cut zucchini and carrot into thin strips. Heat oil in wok, cook chilli and lemon grass, stirring, for about 2 minutes or until fragrant. Add coconut milk and lime leaf, stir until combined and mixture is hot.

2 Add beans, capsicum, zucchini, carrot and broccoli, stir-fry until vegetables are just tender. Add straw mushrooms and basil, stir-fry until hot.

3 Steam or microwave Chinese broccoli until just tender; serve with mixed vegetables.

SERVES 4

store Best made close to serving.
per serving 17.6g fat; 878kJ

Adding coconut milk

Adding straw mushrooms

Serving over bed of Chinese broccoli

stir-fried vegetables with cracked black pepper

PREPARATION TIME 10 MINUTES • COOKING TIME 10 MINUTES

400g bok choy
2 tablespoons oil
2 cloves garlic, crushed
3 medium carrots (360g), sliced
250g beans, halved
1 cup bean sprouts (100g), firmly packed
¹/₄ cup (60ml) water
1 tablespoon fish sauce
1 tablespoon oyster sauce
1 teaspoon sugar
1 teaspoon cracked black peppercorns

1 Tear bok choy into large pieces. Heat oil in wok, stir-fry garlic, carrot and beans until vegetables are almost tender.

2 Stir in bok choy, sprouts, water, sauces, sugar and peppercorns, bring to boil, simmer, uncovered until vegetables are as tender as desired.

SERVES 4

store Best made close to serving.
per serving 10.2g fat; 626kJ

Stir-frying vegetables

Adding sauces to vegetables

deep-fried tofu with peanut sauce

PREPARATION TIME 20 MINUTES (plus standing time) • COOKING TIME 20 MINUTES

**2 x 297g packets tofu, drained
oil for deep-frying**

PEANUT SAUCE
**1 fresh coriander root,
    finely chopped
1 small fresh red chilli,
    finely chopped
2 cloves garlic, crushed
1 tablespoon sugar
2 tablespoons rice vinegar
1/3 cup (90g) smooth
    peanut butter
1/4 cup (60ml) coconut milk**

1 Wrap tofu in 3 sheets of absorbent paper, weigh down with plate; stand 4 hours.

2 Cut tofu into 2cm cubes. Deep-fry cubes in hot oil in batches until well browned; drain on absorbent paper. Serve hot with warm peanut sauce.

peanut sauce Combine coriander root, chilli, garlic, sugar and vinegar in pan, stir over heat until sugar is dissolved. Stir in peanut butter and coconut milk, stir until hot. Serve sprinkled with fresh coriander and chilli, if desired.

SERVES 6

store Sauce can be made 3 days ahead. Store, covered, in refrigerator.
per serving 25g fat; 1343kJ

Weighing down tofu with a plate

Deep-frying tofu cubes

eggplant and dried shrimp salad

PREPARATION TIME 35 MINUTES (plus standing time) • COOKING TIME 8 MINUTES

2 medium eggplants (600g)
2 teaspoons chopped fresh
coriander root
1 teaspoon cracked
black peppercorns
3 cloves garlic, crushed
1 teaspoon sugar
2 tablespoons fish sauce
1 medium fresh red
chilli, chopped
2 tablespoons oil
1/4 cup (60ml) lime juice
1/3 cup (40g) dried shrimp
3 green onions, chopped

1 Peel eggplant, cut into thin strips, place in top half of steamer, cook over boiling water for about 8 minutes or until just tender; drain.

2 Grind coriander, peppercorns and garlic to a paste using mortar and pestle. Combine paste with sugar, sauce, chilli, oil and juice in large bowl. Stir in eggplant; cover, stand 20 minutes.

3 Soak shrimp in cold water in bowl for 10 minutes; drain. Pound shrimp with mortar and pestle. Serve salad sprinkled with shrimp and onion.

SERVES 6

store Can be made a day ahead. Store, covered, in refrigerator
per serving 7g fat; 430kJ

Steaming eggplant strips

Pounding shrimp to a paste

cabbage salad with lime juice dressing

PREPARATION TIME 10 MINUTES • COOKING TIME 10 MINUTES

3 large fresh red chillies
2 tablespoons oil
6 cloves garlic, sliced
6 green onions, sliced
1/2 medium cabbage (750g), shredded
1 tablespoon crushed peanuts

DRESSING
2 tablespoons fish sauce
2 tablespoons lime juice
1/2 cup (125ml) coconut milk

1 Cut chillies into thin strips. Heat oil in pan, cook chilli, garlic and onion separately until lightly browned and crisp; drain on absorbent paper.

2 Add cabbage to pan of boiling water, drain immediately.

3 Combine cabbage and dressing in bowl, mix well. Serve salad topped with stir-fried chilli mixture and peanuts.

dressing Combine all ingredients in bowl; mix well.

SERVES 6

store Salad can be made a day ahead. Store, covered, in refrigerator.
per serving 12.3g fat; 640kJ

Cooking garlic

Combining cabbage and dressing

main courses

Thai food is a taste sensation! The exquisite curry fragrances that emerge from a Thai kitchen come from the sauces, pastes and spices that are used to enhance each special dish. A wok is traditionally used for cooking, but a pan will do just as well for our many quick-and-easy recipes. Here you'll find recipes for seafood, poultry and meat that are usually served as main courses but can also be adapted as entrees and even served at barbecues.

baked fish with sweet and sour sauce

PREPARATION TIME 15 MINUTES • COOKING TIME 45 MINUTES

2 x 400g whole snapper
2 tablespoons fish sauce
1 tablespoon oil

SWEET AND SOUR SAUCE
1 tablespoon oil
2 cloves garlic, crushed
1/4 teaspoon ground ginger
pinch chilli powder
2 tablespoons brown sugar
2 tablespoons white vinegar
2 tablespoons fish sauce
1 large tomato (250g), sliced
1 small yellow capsicum
   (150g), chopped
4 baby carrots, sliced
1/4 cup (60ml) water

1 Cut 4 deep slits into each side of fish, pour fish sauce into slits.

2 Heat oil in heavy baking dish, cook fish on both sides to seal. Bake, covered, in moderate oven for about 30 minutes or until cooked through. Serve with hot sweet and sour sauce.

sweet and sour sauce Heat oil in pan, cook garlic, ginger and chilli, stirring, 1 minute. Add sugar, vinegar and sauce, stir over heat until sugar is dissolved. Stir in remaining ingredients, bring to boil; simmer, covered, for about 3 minutes or until vegetables are just tender.

SERVES 4

store Fish best cooked just before serving. Sauce can be made 3 hours ahead. Store, covered, in refrigerator.
per serving 11g fat; 920kJ

Scoring the fish

Pouring sauce over the fish

Preparing the sweet and sour sauce

steamed mussels with creamy fish filling

PREPARATION TIME 1 HOUR • COOKING TIME 15 MINUTES (plus cooling time)

30 large mussels (1kg)
2 tablespoons oil
1 small brown onion (80g),
finely chopped
2 teaspoons finely chopped
fresh ginger
1 clove garlic, crushed
1 stem fresh lemon grass,
finely chopped
1 teaspoon shrimp paste
500g white fish fillets, chopped
1 egg white
1 tablespoon cream
1 tablespoon chopped fresh
basil leaves
2 small fresh red chillies, sliced

1 Scrub mussels; remove beards. Place mussels in pan, cover with cold water, bring to boil; simmer, covered, for about 3 minutes until mussels begin to open. Drain mussels, rinse under cold water; drain well. Remove and discard top shell from each mussel.

2 Heat oil in pan, cook onion, ginger, garlic and lemon grass, stirring, until onion is soft. Add paste, cook, stirring, for 1 minute; cool.

3 Blend or process fish, egg white and cream until smooth. Combine fish mixture, onion mixture and basil in bowl; mix well. Spoon mixture onto mussels in shells, smooth surface, top with chilli.

4 Place mussels in bamboo steamer in single layer. Cook, covered tightly, over pan of boiling water, for about 3 minutes or until fish mixture is cooked through.

SERVES 6

store Mussels can be prepared a day ahead. Store, covered, in refrigerator.
per serving 10.7g fat; 809kJ

Covering mussels with fish mixture

Steaming the mussels

calamari salad

PREPARATION TIME 50 MINUTES (plus refrigerating time) • COOKING TIME 5 MINUTES (plus cooling time)

1kg baby calamari
1/3 cup (80ml) water
11/2 tablespoons fish sauce
2 tablespoons lime juice
1 small fresh red chilli,
  finely chopped
1 small white onion
  (80g), sliced
1 tablespoon finely chopped
  fresh lemon grass
1 tablespoon chopped fresh
  coriander leaves
1 tablespoon chopped fresh
  mint leaves
8 lettuce leaves

1 Gently pull heads and entrails away from bodies of calamari; discard. Remove clear quills from inside bodies; discard. Remove side flaps and skin from calamari hoods; discard.

2 Cut hoods into 4cm squares, score inside surface of each square using a sharp knife.

3 Combine water, sauce, juice and chilli in pan. Bring to boil, add calamari, simmer, uncovered, for about 2 minutes or until tender, transfer mixture to bowl; cool.

4 Add onion, lemon grass, coriander and mint to bowl. Mix well, cover, refrigerate for at least 1 hour. Serve salad on lettuce.

SERVES 4

store Can be made 6 hours ahead. Store, covered, in refrigerator.
per serving 1.7g fat; 480kJ

Discarding quills from calamari

Scoring inside surface of calamari pieces

squid with red and green capsicum

PREPARATION TIME 30 MINUTES (plus standing time)
COOKING TIME 15 MINUTES

500g squid hoods
1 large green capsicum (350g)
1 large red capsicum (350g)
1 tablespoon oil
4 cloves garlic, sliced
1/3 cup (80ml) water
1 tablespoon palm sugar
1 tablespoon fish sauce
1 tablespoon sweet chilli sauce

1 Cut squid hoods along one side, open out flat. Score inside of hoods using a sharp knife; cut into 2cm x 3cm pieces.

2 Quarter capsicums, remove and discard seeds and membranes. Roast under grill or in a very hot oven, skin-side up, until skin blisters and blackens. Cover capsicum pieces in plastic or paper for 5 minutes, peel away skin. Cut capsicum the same size as squid.

3 Heat oil in wok, stir-fry garlic 1 minute. Add squid, water, sugar and fish sauce, stir-fry for about 2 minutes or until squid curls.

4 Stir in capsicum and chilli sauce, stir-fry until hot.

SERVES 4

store Can be prepared a day ahead. Store, covered, in refrigerator.
per serving 6.7g fat; 822kJ

Scoring inside of squid hoods

Removing skin from capsicum

Adding capsicum to pan

seafood omelette

PREPARATION TIME 25 MINUTES • COOKING TIME 10 MINUTES

3 green onions, chopped
2 cloves garlic, crushed
1 teaspoon ground
black peppercorns
2 tablespoons chopped
fresh coriander root
2 tablespoons oil
350g white fish fillets, chopped
350g cooked king prawns, shelled
1/4 cup (30g) frozen peas
1 tablespoon light soy sauce
1/2 teaspoon fish sauce
1 tablespoon chopped fresh
coriander leaves
1 tablespoon oil, extra
6 eggs, lightly beaten
1 teaspoon cracked
black peppercorns

1 Grind onion, garlic, ground peppercorns and coriander root to a paste using mortar and pestle.

2 Heat oil in pan, cook garlic paste, stirring, for about 2 minutes or until fragrant. Stir in seafood, peas, sauces and fresh coriander, cook, stirring, for 2 minutes; remove from heat.

3 Heat extra oil in pan, pour in combined eggs and cracked peppercorns, cook until omelette is lightly browned underneath and top is almost set.

4 Spoon seafood mixture over half of omelette, fold omelette in half. Cook a further 2 minutes or until mixture is hot and omelette is set.

SERVES 4

store Best made just before serving.
per serving 25.1g fat; 1606kJ

Adding eggs to pan

Folding omelette in half

prawn salad with wine and chilli dressing

PREPARATION TIME 25 MINUTES (plus refrigerating time)

1kg cooked king prawns, shelled
7 cos lettuce leaves

DRESSING
$^1/_4$ cup (60ml) fish sauce
$^1/_3$ cup (80ml) lemon juice
1 tablespoon brown sugar
1 medium fresh red chilli, chopped
$^1/_4$ cup (60ml) dry white wine
1 stem lemon grass, finely chopped
2 tablespoons chopped fresh coriander leaves

1 Combine prawns and dressing in bowl; cover, refrigerate several hours before serving. Serve salad over lettuce.

dressing Combine all ingredients in bowl; mix well.

SERVES 4

store Best made 3 hours ahead. Store, covered, in refrigerator.
per serving 1.3g fat; 732kJ

Adding coriander to dressing

Pouring dressing over prawns

green chicken curry

PREPARATION TIME 25 MINUTES • COOKING TIME 15 MINUTES

750g chicken thigh fillets
200g green beans
1 cup (250ml) coconut cream

GREEN CURRY PASTE

3 small fresh green chillies,
  chopped
3 green onions, chopped
2 cloves garlic, crushed
1/4 cup chopped fresh
  lemon grass
1/4 cup chopped fresh
  coriander leaves
2 tablespoons oil
2 tablespoons water
1 teaspoon shrimp paste
1/2 teaspoon ground cumin
1/4 teaspoon ground turmeric

1 Cut chicken into thin strips. Chop beans. Cook green curry paste
in heated pan, stirring, for about 3 minutes or until fragrant.

2 Add chicken and beans to pan; cook, stirring, for about 5 minutes
or until chicken is tender. Stir in coconut cream; simmer, uncovered,
for about 3 minutes or until slightly thickened.

green curry paste Blend or process all ingredients until smooth.

SERVES 4

store Curry best made just before serving. Paste can be made a week ahead.
Store paste, covered, in refrigerator.
per serving 30.4g fat; 1898kJ

Cooking green curry paste until fragrant

Adding coconut cream

Preparing green curry paste

grilled fish with chilli and coriander sauce

PREPARATION TIME 15 MINUTES • COOKING TIME 10 MINUTES

3 medium fresh red chillies, chopped
1 tablespoon chopped fresh coriander root
3 cloves garlic, crushed
2 teaspoons sugar
4 white fish fillets (800g)
2 tablespoons oil
1 tablespoon fish sauce
1/2 cup (125ml) chicken stock
1 tablespoon lime juice
2 teaspoons cornflour
2 teaspoons water, extra

1 Grind chilli, coriander, garlic and sugar to a paste using mortar and pestle.

2 Brush fish with 1/2 of the oil, grill until just tender.

3 Meanwhile, heat remaining oil in pan, cook chilli mixture, stirring, for 2 minutes. Stir in sauce, stock, juice and blended cornflour and extra water. Stir until mixture boils and thickens. Serve sauce over fish.

SERVES 4

store Best made just before serving.
per serving 15.2g fat; 1353kJ

Brushing fish with oil

Cooking chilli mixture

Adding pineapple

Adding coriander leaves

prawn curry with fresh pineapple and asparagus

PREPARATION TIME 20 MINUTES • COOKING TIME 10 MINUTES

2¹/₂ cups (625ml) coconut cream
¹/₂ medium pineapple (700g), chopped
450g fresh asparagus, chopped
1¹/₂ teaspoons palm sugar
3 teaspoons fish sauce
375g medium cooked prawns, shelled
2 tablespoons fresh coriander leaves
2 green onions, chopped

CURRY PASTE

1¹/₂ teaspoons dried chilli flakes
4 stems fresh lemon grass, chopped
3 teaspoons galangal powder
1 small red onion (100g), chopped
¹/₄ teaspoon shrimp paste
1¹/₂ teaspoons grated lime rind
¹/₄ teaspoon paprika
pinch ground turmeric

1 Combine curry paste and 1 cup of coconut cream in pan, bring to boil, simmer, uncovered, for 3 minutes.

2 Stir in remaining coconut cream, pineapple, asparagus, sugar and sauce. Bring to boil, simmer, uncovered, for 2 minutes.

3 Add prawns and coriander, simmer until hot. Serve curry sprinkled with onion.

curry paste Blend or process all ingredients until combined.

SERVES 4

store Best made just before serving. Paste can be made a week ahead. Store, covered, in refrigerator.

per serving 32.8g fat; 1828kJ

stir-fried seafood with basil

PREPARATION TIME 30 MINUTES • COOKING TIME 10 MINUTES

200g white fish fillets
8 mussels
250g uncooked king prawns
100g squid hoods
2 cloves garlic, crushed
1 large fresh red chilli, chopped
1 tablespoon chopped fresh
coriander root
1/4 cup (60ml) oil
100g scallops
2 tablespoons oyster sauce
2 tablespoons fish sauce
1 medium red capsicum
(200g), sliced
8 green onions, chopped
1/3 cup shredded fresh
basil leaves

1 Chop fish into bite-sized pieces. Scrub mussels, remove beards. Shell prawns, leaving tails intact. Cut squid into 6cm squares, score inside surface of squid using a sharp knife.

2 Grind garlic, chilli and coriander to a paste using mortar and pestle. Heat oil in wok, cook paste stirring, for about 1 minute, or until fragrant.

3 Add all seafood to wok, stir-fry until seafood is tender.

4 Stir in sauces, capsicum, onion and basil, stir-fry for 2 minutes.

SERVES 4

store Seafood can be prepared a day ahead. Best made just before serving. Store, covered, in refrigerator.
per serving 18g fat; 1406kJ

Preparing seafood

Stir-frying spice paste

Stir-frying seafood

steamed minced pork cups

PREPARATION TIME 25 MINUTES • COOKING TIME 20 MINUTES (plus cooling time)

250g minced pork
180g minced chicken
170g can crab meat, drained
1/4 cup (60ml) coconut milk
4 green onions, chopped
1 tablespoon chopped fresh coriander leaves
1 stem fresh lemon grass, chopped
3 cloves garlic, crushed
2 tablespoons fish sauce
1/2 teaspoon palm sugar
1/4 teaspoon cracked black peppercorns
2 eggs, separated
4 small green cucumbers (520g), chopped
2 cups (200g) bean sprouts
2 small red capsicums (300g), chopped

1 Blend or process pork, chicken, crab, coconut milk, onion, coriander, lemon grass, garlic, sauce, sugar and peppercorns until combined; transfer mixture to bowl.

2 Beat egg whites with 1 of the egg yolks in small bowl with electric mixer until thick and creamy. Fold into pork mixture.

3 Spoon pork mixture into 6 (1/2 cup/125ml capacity) ungreased bowls, press in firmly, smooth tops. Brush tops with remaining egg yolk.

4 Place bowls in bamboo steamer, cook, covered, over boiling water for about 20 minutes or until cooked through; cool. Turn out cups. Serve over combined cucumber, sprouts and capsicum.

SERVES 6

store Can be prepared a day ahead. Store, covered, in refrigerator. Uncooked cups suitable to freeze.
per serving 9.1g fat; 810.7kJ

Spooning pork mixture into bowls

Steaming the bowls

snapper cutlets with red curry paste

PREPARATION TIME 20 MINUTES • COOKING TIME 15 MINUTES

1/4 cup (60ml) oil
4 snapper cutlets (1kg)
1/2 cup (125ml) coconut milk
1 tablespoon chopped fresh coriander leaves

RED CURRY PASTE
2 small fresh red chillies, chopped
1 tablespoon chopped fresh coriander root
2 cloves garlic, crushed
1 teaspoon shrimp paste
2 teaspoons chopped fresh lemon grass
1 teaspoon ground cumin
2 teaspoons paprika
1 medium red onion (170g), chopped
1/4 cup (60ml) lime juice

1 Heat oil in pan, cook fish until tender. Remove from pan.

2 Pour excess oil from pan, add paste; cook, stirring, for about 3 minutes or until fragrant. Stir in milk, bring to boil, simmer, uncovered, until slightly thickened. Serve over fish, sprinkle with coriander.

red curry paste Blend all ingredients until combined.

SERVES 4

store Best made just before serving. Paste can be made a week ahead. Store, covered, in refrigerator.
per serving 25.2g fat; 1724kJ

Cooking the fish

Adding coconut milk to curry paste

Combining chicken and coconut milk

Pouring sauce over chicken

chicken and peanut curry

PREPARATION TIME 20 MINUTES • COOKING TIME 25 MINUTES

8 chicken thigh fillets (875g)
400ml coconut cream
1 tablespoon chopped fresh
  coriander leaves

COCONUT AND PEANUT SAUCE
1/2 cup (75g) peanuts
1 clove garlic, crushed
2 teaspoons ground cumin
1 teaspoon ground coriander
1 small fresh red chilli,
  finely chopped
1/2 teaspoon shrimp paste
1 tablespoon light soy sauce
2 teaspoons sugar
1 tablespoon lime juice

1 Combine chicken and coconut cream in pan, bring to boil; simmer, uncovered, for about 20 minutes, or until chicken is tender. Strain chicken, reserve 1 cup liquid.

2 Slice chicken, arrange on serving plate or bowl, pour over coconut and peanut sauce. Sprinkle with fresh coriander.

coconut and peanut sauce Blend or process peanuts until coarsely chopped. Combine garlic, cumin, ground coriander and chilli in pan, stir over heat for about 1 minute or until fragrant. Add reserved liquid, nuts, paste, sauce, sugar and juice, stir until combined and hot.

SERVES 4

store Can be made 1 hour ahead. Store chicken and sauce separately, covered, in refrigerator. Suitable to freeze.
per serving 37.3g fat; 2284kJ

baked garlic quail

PREPARATION TIME 15 MINUTES (plus refrigerating time)
COOKING TIME 25 MINUTES

4 quail (780g)
4 cloves garlic, crushed
1/4 cup (60g) sambal oelek
2 tablespoons honey
2 tablespoons light soy sauce
2 teaspoons brown sugar
2 tablespoons oil

1 Cut quail in half through centres. Combine garlic, sambal oelek, honey, sauce, sugar and oil in bowl. Add quail, stir well. Cover, refrigerate overnight.

2 Place quail on rack over baking dish. Bake in moderate oven for 15 minutes; increase temperature to hot, cook further 10 minutes or until quail are crisp and tender.

SERVES 4

store Quail can be prepared 2 days ahead. Store, covered, in refrigerator. Uncooked quail suitable to freeze.
per serving 14.2g fat; 1141kJ

Adding quail to marinade

Quail ready to bake

baked duck and mandarin salad

PREPARATION TIME 25 MINUTES (plus refrigerating time) • COOKING TIME 1¹/₂ HOURS (plus cooling time)

1.6kg duckling
60g butter, melted
¹/₄ teaspoon paprika
310g can mandarin segments
2 tablespoons rice vinegar
2 tablespoons oyster sauce
2 tablespoons sesame oil
2 green onions, chopped
¹/₂ cup (35g) shredded
   coconut, toasted

1 Place duck on rack over baking
   dish, brush all over with
   combined butter and paprika.
   Bake duck in moderate oven for
   about 1¹/₂ hours or until well
   browned and tender, frequently
   brushing with butter mixture.
   Prick duck skin with fork when
   beginning to brown. Remove
   duck from oven; cool. Remove
   flesh from bones; cut flesh into
   thin strips.

2 Drain mandarins, reserve syrup.
   Combine duck, reserved syrup,
   vinegar, sauce and oil in bowl;
   cover, refrigerate several hours
   or overnight.

3 Stir mandarins, onion and
   toasted coconut through
   duck mixture.

SERVES 4

store Can be prepared 2 days
ahead. Store, covered,
in refrigerator.
per serving 87g fat; 4158kJ

Cutting duck flesh into strips

Adding toasted coconut

Cut chicken into strips

Adding coconut cream

chilli chicken with basil and coconut cream

PREPARATION TIME 20 MINUTES • COOKING TIME 15 MINUTES

500g chicken breast fillets
2 tablespoons oil
1 medium brown onion (150g), finely chopped
2 tablespoons finely chopped small fresh red chillies
1 cup (80g) shredded fresh basil leaves
2 tablespoons fish sauce
1 teaspoon chopped fresh coriander root
1¹/₂ teaspoons sugar
1 cup (250ml) coconut cream

1 Remove excess fat from chicken, cut chicken into 1cm strips.

2 Heat oil in wok, stir-fry onion and chilli until onion is soft.

3 Add chicken, stir-fry until chicken is tender. Add basil, sauce, coriander and sugar, stir-fry for 1 minute.

4 Add coconut cream, stir until mixture is hot.

SERVES 4

store Best made just before serving.
per serving 25.2g fat; 1558kJ

chicken in coconut milk

PREPARATION TIME 15 MINUTES • COOKING TIME 30 MINUTES

**4 single chicken breast fillets
  (680g)**
3 cups (750ml) coconut milk
1 teaspoon dried chilli flakes
2 tablespoons chopped peanuts
1/4 teaspoon black peppercorns
**2 stems fresh lemon grass,
  chopped**
4 green onions, chopped
2 cloves garlic, crushed
1 tablespoon brown sugar
1 teaspoon shrimp paste
2 teaspoons oil
1 cup (250ml) coconut milk, extra

1 Combine chicken and coconut milk in pan, bring to boil, simmer; covered, for 20 minutes. Drain chicken; discard coconut milk.

2 Meanwhile, blend chilli, peanuts, peppercorns, lemon grass, onion, garlic, sugar and paste until well combined.

3 Heat oil in pan, cook peanut mixture, stirring, for about 2 minutes or until fragrant. Stir in extra coconut milk and chicken, stir until hot.

SERVES 4

store Can be prepared a day ahead. Store, covered, in refrigerator.
per serving 30.6g fat; 1894kJ

Preparing peanut mixture

Cooking peanut mixture until fragrant

chicken and baby corn

PREPARATION TIME 25 MINUTES • COOKING TIME 15 MINUTES

750g chicken thigh fillets
425g can baby corn, drained
1 tablespoon oil
4 cloves garlic, thinly sliced
2 small fresh red chillies,
thinly sliced
1 tablespoon oil, extra
1 medium brown onion
(150g), chopped
1 medium red pepper
(200g), sliced
10 leaves Chinese broccoli,
shredded
1 tablespoon fish sauce
1 tablespoon light soy sauce
1 teaspoon grated fresh ginger

1 Cut chicken into thin strips. Cut baby corn in half lengthways. Heat oil in wok, stir-fry garlic and chilli until lightly browned; remove from wok.

2 Add chicken to wok in several batches, stir-fry until tender; remove from wok.

3 Add extra oil to wok, stir-fry onion and pepper for 1 minute. Return chicken to wok with corn, broccoli, sauces and ginger, stir-fry until hot. Serve topped with garlic and chillies.

SERVES 4

store Best made just before serving.
per serving 17.9g fat; 1487kJ

Stir-frying garlic and chilli

Adding sauces to pan

chicken and toasted rice salad

PREPARATION TIME 40 MINUTES (plus cooling time) • COOKING TIME 20 MINUTES (plus standing time)

1 cup (250ml) chicken stock
2 single chicken breast
fillets (340g)
2 tablespoons long grain rice
4 green onions, chopped
2 large fresh red chillies,
chopped
2 tablespoons chopped fresh
mint leaves
1 tablespoon chopped fresh
coriander leaves
1 tablespoon chopped fresh
lemon grass
1 cos lettuce
¼ cup (60ml) lime juice
1 tablespoon fish sauce
1 teaspoon sugar

1 Bring stock to boil in a pan, add chicken, simmer, covered, until just tender. Stand chicken in stock for 10 minutes; drain chicken; reserve 1 tablespoon stock. Discard remaining stock. Chop chicken finely; cool.

2 Place rice in dry pan, stir over heat for about 5 minutes or until lightly browned. Grind rice in batches to a fine powder using mortar and pestle.

3 Combine chicken, rice, onion, chilli, mint, coriander and lemon grass in bowl; serve in lettuce leaves.

4 Pour over combined juice, sauce, sugar and reserved stock.

SERVES 4

storage Salad can be prepared a day ahead. Store, covered, in refrigerator.
per serving 2.8g fat; 717kJ

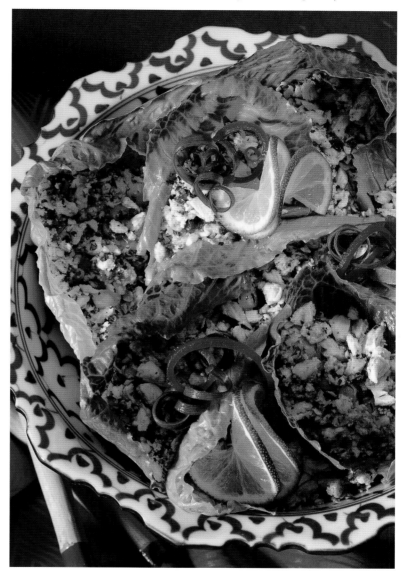

Chopping chicken finely

Grinding rice to a fine powder

beef curry with red and green chillies

PREPARATION TIME 40 MINUTES • COOKING TIME 25 MINUTES

1kg beef rump steak
1 small fresh red chilli
1 small fresh green chilli
2 cups (500ml) coconut milk
1/4 cup (60ml) coconut cream
2 teaspoons fish sauce
2 tablespoons raw sugar
4 green onions, chopped
2 tablespoons oil

CURRY PASTE

2 small fresh red chillies, chopped
3 cloves garlic, crushed
1 teaspoon chopped fresh
  lemon grass
1 teaspoon grated lime rind
1 teaspoon dried galangal
1/4 teaspoon ground cardamom
2 green onions, chopped
1/2 teaspoon cracked
  black peppercorns
2 teaspoons chopped fresh
  coriander root
1/2 teaspoon shrimp paste
2 teaspoons lime juice

1 Cut steak into 5cm slices. Cut chillies into thin strips. Heat coconut milk in pan, add steak, bring to boil; simmer, uncovered, for about 15 minutes or until steak is tender.

2 Heat coconut cream in separate pan, add curry paste, simmer, uncovered, for about 1 minute or until fragrant.

3 Stir paste mixture into steak mixture, bring to boil; simmer, uncovered, until liquid is almost evaporated. Stir in sauce, sugar and onion.

4 Heat oil in separate pan, cook chilli, stirring, for about 2 minutes or until crisp. Sprinkle cooked chilli over curry just before serving.

curry paste Grind all ingredients to a paste using mortar and pestle.

SERVES 6

store Curry best made just before serving. Paste can be made a week ahead. Store, covered, in refrigerator.
per serving 39.1g fat; 2264kJ

Adding steak to coconut milk

Adding curry paste to steak mixture

Preparing curry paste

dry beef curry with onions and peanuts

PREPARATION TIME 30 MINUTES • COOKING TIME 1¹/₄ HOURS

Adding peanuts to pan

Adding onions to pan

Preparing curry paste

1kg beef chuck steak, chopped
3 cups (750ml) coconut milk
1 cup (150g) finely ground peanuts
1 tablespoon fish sauce
2 teaspoons tamarind sauce
6 baby onions (150g)
¹/₄ teaspoon ground cloves
¹/₄ teaspoon ground cardamom
¹/₄ teaspoon ground cinnamon
1¹/₂ tablespoons lime juice
1 teaspoon palm sugar

CURRY PASTE
2 teaspoons dried chilli flakes
1 medium red onion (170g), chopped
3 cloves garlic, crushed
2 tablespoons chopped fresh lemon grass
1 teaspoon galangal powder
2 teaspoons chopped fresh coriander root
1 teaspoon grated lime rind
¹/₂ teaspoon shrimp paste
1 dried kaffir lime leaf
1 teaspoon paprika
¹/₂ teaspoon ground turmeric
¹/₂ teaspoon cumin seeds
2 teaspoons oil, approximately

1 Combine beef, coconut milk and peanuts in pan, bring to the boil, simmer, covered, 1 hour, stirring occasionally.

2 Stir in curry paste, sauces, onions, spices, juice and sugar, simmer, uncovered, 10 minutes.

curry paste Blend or process all ingredients with enough oil to form a paste consistency.

SERVES 6

store Recipe can be prepared a day ahead. Paste can be made a week ahead. Store, covered, in refrigerator. Suitable to freeze.
per serving 50.4g fat; 2771kJ

Cutting quail into portions

Deep-frying quail

quail with fresh chilli and basil

PREPARATION TIME 15 MINUTES • COOKING TIME 15 MINUTES

4 quail (780g)
oil for deep-frying
1 clove garlic, crushed
1 small fresh red chilli,
  finely chopped
1 tablespoon oyster sauce
1 tablespoon fish sauce
2 tablespoons shredded fresh
  basil leaves

1 Cut quail in half, cut away backbone. Cut each quail half into 3 portions.

2 Deep-fry quail pieces in hot oil in wok until well browned and tender; drain on absorbent paper.

3 Drain oil from wok, leave 1 tablespoon oil in wok. Add garlic, chilli and sauces to wok, cook, stirring, for 1 minute. Return quail to wok, stir until hot.

4 Stir in basil.

SERVES 4

store Best made just before serving.
per serving 51.7g fat; 2338kJ

barbecued chicken with sweet vinegar sauce

PREPARATION TIME 45 MINUTES (plus refrigerating time) • COOKING TIME 25 MINUTES (plus cooling time)

1kg chicken thigh fillets
1/2 cup (125ml) coconut milk

PASTE
4 cloves garlic, crushed
1 teaspoon cracked
**   black peppercorns**
2 teaspoons sugar
2 teaspoons ground turmeric
2 teaspoons paprika
1 tablespoon chopped fresh
**   coriander root**
1 teaspoon curry powder
2 small fresh red chillies, chopped
1 tablespoon oil

SWEET VINEGAR SAUCE
1 small fresh red chilli, chopped
2 cloves garlic, crushed
1/2 cup (125ml) white vinegar
2 tablespoons raw sugar

1 Cut thigh fillets in half, combine with paste in bowl; cover, refrigerate several hours or overnight.

2 Grill chicken until tender, basting frequently with coconut milk. Serve with sweet vinegar sauce.

paste Grind all ingredients to a paste using mortar and pestle.

sweet vinegar sauce Grind chilli and garlic to a paste using mortar and pestle. Combine vinegar and sugar in pan, stir over heat, without boiling, until sugar is dissolved. Bring to boil, simmer, uncovered, without stirring, until syrup just begins to colour; remove from heat, cool slightly. Stir in chilli and garlic paste.

SERVES 4

store Recipe can be prepared 2 days ahead, paste a week ahead and sauce 6 hours ahead. Store, covered, in refrigerator. Uncooked chicken suitable to freeze.
per serving 23.1g fat; 1997kJ

Combining chicken and paste

Grilling chicken until tender

beef curry with bamboo shoots

PREPARATION TIME 30 MINUTES (plus standing time) • COOKING TIME 15 MINUTES

2 tablespoons oil
1.2kg beef rump steak, thinly sliced
400g can bamboo shoots,
  drained, sliced
2 small fresh red chillies,
  chopped
2 small fresh green chillies,
  chopped
2 tablespoons fish sauce
1 dried kaffir lime leaf
1 teaspoon brown sugar
2 tablespoons chopped fresh
  basil leaves

CURRY PASTE

5 dried red chillies
1 tablespoon chopped
  dried galangal
1 tablespoon chopped dried
  kaffir lime peel
1 cup (250g) water
2 green onions, chopped

2 cloves garlic, crushed
2 teaspoons grated lemon rind
1 tablespoon finely chopped
  fresh lemon grass
1 teaspoon finely chopped
  fresh ginger

1 Heat oil in large wok, stir-fry steak in batches until browned all over. Return steak to pan. Add 1/4 cup curry paste, stir for 2 minutes.

2 Add bamboo shoots, chilli, sauce, lime leaf and sugar; stir-fry until steak is tender. Stir in basil.

curry paste Combine chilli, galangal and peel in bowl, cover with water; cover, stand several hours. Drain peel mixture, reserve 1/2 cup liquid. Blend or process peel mixture, reserved liquid, onion, garlic, rind, lemon grass and ginger until smooth.

SERVES 8

store Curry best made close to serving. Paste can be made 2 weeks ahead. Store, covered, in refrigerator. Curry suitable to freeze; paste not suitable.
per serving 14.9g fat; 1159kJ

Adding curry paste to wok

Stirring in basil

Preparing curry paste

deep-fried wings with mince stuffing

PREPARATION TIME 50 MINUTES • COOKING TIME 15 MINUTES (plus cooling time)

12 large chicken wings (1.3kg)
500g minced chicken
2 green onions, chopped
2 teaspoons chopped
 fresh ginger
2 cloves garlic, crushed
1 small fresh red chilli, chopped
1 tablespoon cornflour
cornflour, extra
1 egg, lightly beaten
1 cup (100g) packaged
 breadcrumbs
oil for deep-frying

SWEET CHILLI PEANUT SAUCE
¹/₂ cup (110g) sugar
2 tablespoons water
2 tablespoons white vinegar
1 tablespoon chopped peanuts
1 small fresh red chilli, chopped

1 Holding end of large third joint of wings, trim around bone with knife. Cut, scrape and push meat down to middle joint, without cutting skin. Twist bone and remove; discard bone.

2 Blend or process mince, onion, ginger, garlic, chilli and cornflour until combined. Using fingers, fill cavities of wings with mince mixture, secure ends with toothpicks.

3 Toss wings in extra cornflour, shake away excess cornflour. Dip into egg, then breadcrumbs.

4 Deep-fry wings in hot oil until well browned and tender; drain on absorbent paper. Serve with sweet chilli peanut sauce.

sweet chilli peanut sauce Combine sugar and water in pan, stir over heat until sugar is dissolved. Bring to boil, simmer, uncovered, for 2 minutes; cool. Stir in vinegar, peanuts and chilli.

MAKES 12

store Can be prepared 2 days ahead. Store, covered, in refrigerator. Uncooked crumbed wings suitable to freeze.
per wing 23.4g fat; 1512kJ

Preparing chicken wings

Filling cavities with mince mixture

Lightly browning almonds

Stirring in coriander and basil

chicken and almond stir-fry

PREPARATION TIME 15 MINUTES • COOKING TIME 10 MINUTES

300g chicken breast fillets
80g green beans
1/4 cup (60ml) oil
2/3 cup (110g) blanched
almond kernels
1 teaspoon curry paste
2 tablespoons fish sauce
2 tablespoons oyster sauce
1 small fresh red chilli,
finely chopped
1 tablespoon manjo mirin
1 tablespoon chopped fresh
coriander leaves
1 tablespoon chopped fresh
basil leaves

1 Thinly slice chicken. Cut beans into 2cm lengths.

2 Heat half the oil in wok, stir-fry almonds until lightly browned; remove almonds from wok; reserve.

3 Reheat remaining oil in wok, add chicken, stir-fry 1 minute. Add beans, paste, sauces, chilli, mirin and almonds, stir-fry until chicken is just tender; stir in coriander and basil.

SERVES 4

store Best made just before serving.
per serving 31.5g fat; 1665kJ

beef with oyster sauce

PREPARATION TIME 15 MINUTES • COOKING TIME 10 MINUTES

400g bok choy
250g Chinese broccoli
500g beef rump steak
2 tablespoons oil
2 cloves garlic, crushed
150g snow peas
425g can baby corn, drained
6 green onions, chopped
2 tablespoons oyster sauce
1 tablespoon fish sauce
1 tablespoon sugar

1 Break bok choy and broccoli into large pieces, steam or microwave until just tender; drain well.

2 Cut steak into thin strips. Heat oil in wok, stir-fry garlic and steak until steak is just browned.

3 Add peas, corn, onion, sauces and sugar, stir-fry until peas are just tender. Serve over bok choy and broccoli.

SERVES 4

store Recipe best made just before serving.
per serving 19g fat; 1503kJ

Steaming bok choy and broccoli

Adding garlic to pan

Adding chopped green onions

stir-fried steak with green beans

PREPARATION TIME 15 MINUTES • COOKING TIME 10 MINUTES

180g green beans
1 tablespoon oil
1 medium brown onion
  (150g), chopped
2 cloves garlic, crushed
1 large fresh green chilli,
  chopped
1 large fresh red chilli, chopped
1 tablespoon oil, extra
500g beef rump steak,
  thinly sliced
1 tablespoon fish sauce
1 tablespoon chopped fresh
  coriander leaves
1 teaspoon sugar

1 Slice beans diagonally. Heat oil in wok, stir-fry onion, garlic, chilli and beans until beans are just tender; remove from wok.

2 Add extra oil to wok, add steak in batches, stir-fry until tender.

3 Return steak and bean mixture to wok with sauce, coriander and sugar, stir-fry for about 2 minutes, or until hot.

SERVES 4

store Best made close to serving.
per serving 18.1g fat; 1250kJ

Stir-frying beans until tender

Adding sauce, coriander and sugar

red chicken curry

PREPARATION TIME 30 MINUTES • COOKING TIME 15 MINUTES

2 tablespoons oil
4 green onions, chopped
750g chicken thigh fillets,
   chopped
2 tablespoons fish sauce
1 cup (250ml) coconut milk

CURRY PASTE
1 small red onion (100g), chopped
3 cloves garlic
2 tablespoons chopped fresh
   lemon grass
3 teaspoons chopped fresh
   coriander root
2 teaspoons dried chilli flakes
1 teaspoon galangal powder
1 teaspoon grated lime rind
$1/2$ teaspoon shrimp paste
1 dried kaffir lime leaf
3 teaspoons paprika
$1/2$ teaspoon ground turmeric
$1/2$ teaspoon cumin seeds
3 teaspoons oil

1 Heat oil in wok, cook $1/3$ cup of the curry paste and green onion, stirring, for about 2 minutes or until fragrant. Reserve remaining curry paste for another use.

2 Add chicken in batches, stir-fry until just tender. Return chicken to wok.

3 Stir in sauce and coconut milk, bring to boil, simmer, uncovered, until mixture is hot.

curry paste Blend or process all ingredients until smooth.

SERVES 6

store Can be made a day ahead. Curry paste can be made a week ahead. Store, covered, in refrigerator. Suitable to freeze.
per serving 24.1g fat; 1420kJ

Stir-frying curry paste and green onion

Adding chicken to wok

beef and mushroom salad

PREPARATION TIME 25 MINUTES (plus standing time) • COOKING TIME 10 MINUTES (plus cooling time)

**60g (2 cups) dried shiitake
  mushrooms**
600g piece beef rump steak
2 tablespoons oil
**1 medium red capsicum
  (200g), sliced**
1/2 cup (75g) roasted cashews
**9 large English spinach leaves,
  shredded**

DRESSING
2 tablespoons sesame oil
2 tablespoons fish sauce
2 tablespoons sweet sherry
2 tablespoons oyster sauce

1 Place mushrooms in bowl, cover with warm water, stand 20 minutes. Drain mushrooms, discard stems, cut caps into thin slices.

2 Trim excess fat from steak. Heat oil in pan, cook steak until browned on both sides and medium rare; cool. Cut steak into thin strips.

3 Combine steak, mushrooms, pepper, nuts and spinach in bowl. Add dressing; toss well.

dressing Combine all ingredients in bowl; mix well.

SERVES 4

store Steak can be prepared a day ahead. Store, covered, in refrigerator.
per serving 38.8g fat; 2340kJ

Slicing steak and mushrooms

Combining steak and other ingredients

Mixing together dressing

lamb with basil and vegetables

PREPARATION TIME 20 MINUTES • COOKING TIME 15 MINUTES

Preparing vegetables

Stir-frying brown onions

Adding remaining ingredients

2 cloves garlic
2 large fresh red chillies
1 medium carrot (120g)
1 medium brown onion (150g)
2 tablespoons oil
1¹/₂ tablespoons tandoori curry paste
500g lamb fillet, thinly sliced
230g can bamboo shoots, drained, sliced
4 green onions, chopped
¹/₃ cup shredded fresh basil leaves
1 tablespoon fish sauce

1 Cut garlic, chillies and carrot into thin strips. Cut brown onion into wedges.

2 Heat ¹/₂ the oil in wok, stir-fry garlic and chilli until lightly browned; remove from wok. Reheat wok, stir-fry brown onion until soft, remove from wok.

3 Add remaining oil to wok, heat oil, cook curry paste 1 minute. Stir-fry lamb in batches until tender.

4 Return lamb and onion to wok with remaining ingredients, stir-fry until hot. Serve lamb mixture topped with garlic and chilli.

SERVES 4

store Best made close to serving.
per serving 15.3g fat; 1156kJ

minced pork salad with ginger and mint (larb)

PREPARATION TIME 20 MINUTES • COOKING TIME 10 MINUTES (plus cooling time)

500g pork fillet, chopped
1 tablespoon oil
1 tablespoon water
1/4 cup (60ml) lime juice
2 tablespoons fish sauce
2 small fresh red chillies, chopped
1 small brown onion (80g),
   finely sliced
4 green onions, chopped
1/4 cup (35g) peanuts
1 tablespoon grated fresh ginger
2 tablespoons chopped fresh
   mint leaves
2 tablespoons fresh
   coriander leaves
8 cos lettuce leaves
1 tablespoon chopped
   peanuts, extra
20g sliced fresh ginger, extra
2 tablespoons fresh coriander
   leaves, extra

1 Process pork until finely minced. Heat oil in pan, cook pork and water, stirring, until pork is tender.

2 Remove pork from heat, stir in juice, sauce and chilli; cool.

3 Combine pork mixture with brown onion, green onion, peanuts, ginger, mint and coriander in bowl. Serve pork salad over lettuce, sprinkled with extra chopped peanuts, extra ginger and extra coriander.

SERVES 4

store Can be made a day ahead. Store, covered, in refrigerator.
per serving 12.5g fat; 1108kJ

Stirring in lime juice

Adding peanuts to pork mixture

peppered prawns with leek

PREPARATION TIME 20 MINUTES • COOKING TIME 10 MINUTES

1 large leek (500g)
500g uncooked king prawns
2 tablespoons oil
1 clove garlic, crushed
1 tablespoon fish sauce
1 teaspoon brown sugar
1 teaspoon cracked
  black peppercorns
1 teaspoon chopped fresh
  coriander leaves

1 Cut leek in half, cut into 3cm pieces. Add leek to pan of boiling water, boil until just tender; drain.

2 Shell prawns, leaving tails intact. Cut along centre back of prawns, remove vein, flatten prawns slightly.

3 Heat oil in wok, stir-fry prawns and garlic for 2 minutes. Add sauce, sugar and peppercorns, stir-fry until prawns are tender. Serve prawns over leek, pour over liquid, sprinkle with coriander.

SERVES 4

store Best made just before serving; prawns can be prepared 6 hours ahead. Store, covered, in refrigerator.
per serving 10.2g fat; 667kJ

Slicing leek

De-veining prawns

lamb fillet in chilli and coconut milk

PREPARATION TIME 35 MINUTES (plus standing time) • COOKING TIME 20 MINUTES

800g lamb fillet
1 tablespoon oil
3 small fresh red chillies, chopped
1¹/₂ cups (375ml) coconut milk
2 tablespoons fish sauce
1 teaspoon palm sugar
2 tablespoons lime juice
¹/₂ cup (75g) peanuts, finely
  chopped
2 tablespoons chopped
  fresh coriander leaves

CURRY PASTE

3 dried chillies, chopped
1 dried kaffir lime leaf
¹/₂ teaspoon galangal powder
1 stem fresh lemon grass, chopped
1 teaspoon shrimp powder
¹/₃ cup (80ml) boiling water
4 green onions, chopped
2 cloves garlic, crushed
¹/₄ teaspoon ground coriander
1 tablespoon fish sauce
2 tablespoons crunchy
  peanut butter

1 Cut each lamb fillet into 3 portions, pound each piece with mallet until 5mm thick. Heat oil in pan, cook lamb until browned on both sides; remove from pan.

2 Combine 2 tablespoons of curry paste with chilli in pan, stir over heat for about 2 minutes or until fragrant.

3 Add coconut milk, sauce, sugar, juice and peanuts, stir until boiling. Add lamb to pan, simmer, covered, for about 5 minutes or until lamb is tender. Stir in coriander.

curry paste Combine chilli, lime leaf, galangal, lemon grass, shrimp powder and water in bowl; stand 20 minutes. Drain chilli mixture, discard liquid. Blend or process chilli mixture with remaining ingredients until a coarse paste forms.

SERVES 4

store Can be made several hours ahead. Paste can be made 2 weeks ahead. Store, covered, in refrigerator; store paste, covered, in refrigerator. Cooked recipe suitable to freeze.
per serving 49g fat; 2865kJ

Cooking lamb until browned on both sides

Cooking curry paste and chilli until fragrant

Stirring in coriander

sweet and sour pork spare ribs

PREPARATION TIME 15 MINUTES • COOKING TIME 30 MINUTES

1 tablespoon oil
2 cloves garlic, crushed
1/2 medium red onion
   (85g), chopped
2 tablespoons sugar
2 tablespoons lime juice
1/4 cup (60ml) pineapple juice
2 teaspoons fish sauce
1 tablespoon oyster sauce
1/3 cup (80ml) tomato sauce
1 tablespoon sweet chilli sauce
1 tablespoon white vinegar
1kg pork spare ribs

1 Heat oil in pan, cook garlic and onion, stirring, until onion is soft. Stir in combined sugar, juices, sauces and vinegar; bring to boil, simmer, uncovered, 2 minutes or until slightly thickened.

2 Place spare ribs on rack over baking dish, brush with sweet and sour sauce. Bake in hot oven for 10 minutes, reduce heat to moderately hot, bake about 15 minutes or until pork is crisp and cooked through. Turn and baste ribs several times during cooking.

SERVES 4

store Sauce can be made 2 days ahead. Store sauce, covered, in refrigerator. Cooked and uncooked ribs suitable to freeze.
per serving 23.5g fat; 1796kJ

Preparing sweet and sour sauce

Brushing spare ribs with sauce

Adding pork to pan

Adding eggplant

pork curry with eggplant

PREPARATION TIME 30 MINUTES • COOKING TIME 20 MINUTES

750g pork fillet
1/4 cup (60ml) coconut cream
21/2 cups (625ml) coconut milk
1 medium eggplant
   (300g), chopped
1 tablespoon fish sauce
11/2 teaspoons grated
   fresh ginger
2 teaspoons palm sugar
3 small fresh green
   chillies, sliced
3 small fresh red chillies, sliced
1/4 cup fresh basil leaves

CURRY PASTE
2 teaspoons dried chilli flakes
1 medium red onion
   (170g), chopped
3 cloves garlic, crushed
2 tablespoons chopped fresh
   lemon grass
1 teaspoon galangal powder
2 teaspoons chopped fresh
   coriander root

1 teaspoon grated lime rind
1/2 teaspoon shrimp paste
1 dried kaffir lime leaf
1 teaspoon paprika
1/2 teaspoon ground turmeric
1/2 teaspoon cumin seeds
2 teaspoons oil, approximately

1 Cut pork into 2cm slices, then cut slices in half. Combine coconut cream and curry paste in pan, cook for 1 minute or until fragrant. Add pork, cook 5 minutes.

2 Stir in coconut milk, eggplant, sauce, ginger, sugar and chilli. Bring to the boil, simmer, covered, until pork is tender. Stir in basil.

curry paste Blend or process all ingredients with enough oil to form a paste consistency.

SERVES 6

store Can be prepared a day ahead. Paste can be made a week ahead. Store, covered, in refrigerator.
per serving 30.3g fat; 1790kJ

rice and noodles

Rice is the staple of the Thai diet. Freshly steamed rice is served with curries and soups as part of a meal, while more elaborate preparations – fried rice as well as fried noodles – are served as light meals in their own right. Rice, when served as an accompaniment, is cooked using the absorption method and our steamed jasmine rice recipe will ensure fluffy, fragrant rice every time.

noodles with garlic, beef and broccoli

PREPARATION TIME 15 MINUTES (plus standing time) • COOKING TIME 10 MINUTES

250g rice vermicelli
450g beef rump steak
2 tablespoons oil
2 tablespoons dark soy sauce
5 cloves garlic, sliced
700g broccoli, chopped
1 tablespoon oyster sauce
1 tablespoon cornflour
3/4 cup (180ml) water
1/4 cup (60ml) white vinegar
1 tablespoon sugar
1 small red chilli, chopped
1 small green chilli, chopped

1 Soak vermicelli in warm water for 15 minutes, drain well. Slice steak into 1cm x 5cm strips.

2 Heat 1 tablespoon of the oil in wok, stir-fry vermicelli and soy sauce for 2 minutes, remove from wok.

3 Heat remaining oil in wok, stir-fry garlic and steak until steak is browned all over.

4 Stir in broccoli, oyster sauce, blended cornflour and water, vinegar and sugar, stir-fry until mixture boils and thickens. Serve broccoli mixture over noodles sprinkled with chillies.

SERVES 4

store Best made close to serving. Store, covered, in refrigerator.
per serving 18.2g fat; 2011kJ

Slicing steak into strips

Stir-frying vermicelli and soy sauce

Adding steak to pan

fried rice sticks with coconut sauce

PREPARATION TIME 20 MINUTES (plus standing time)
COOKING TIME 20 MINUTES

200g rice sticks
1 medium carrot (120g)
1 tablespoon oil
2 cloves garlic, crushed
1 medium brown onion
  (150g), chopped
250g pork fillet, thinly sliced
2 cups (500ml) coconut milk
1/2 cup (125ml) coconut cream
2 teaspoons palm sugar
2 teaspoons fish sauce
2 teaspoons tamarind sauce
1 tablespoon chopped
  fresh chives
100g firm tofu, chopped
2 tablespoons fresh coriander
  leaves

1 Place rice sticks in bowl; cover with hot water, stand 15 minutes.

2 Chop carrot into thin strips. Heat oil in wok, cook garlic, onion and pork until pork is browned and tender.

3 Stir in coconut milk, coconut cream, sugar, sauces and carrot, simmer 5 minutes. Remove 1/3 cup liquid from wok.

4 Stir in drained rice sticks; cook 5 minutes or until tender. Stir in chives. Place rice sticks on serving dish, spoon over reserved liquid. Serve topped with tofu and coriander.

SERVES 4

store Best made close to serving time.
per serving 43g fat; 2633kJ

Adding carrots to pan

Adding coriander and tofu

steamed jasmine rice

PREPARATION TIME 5 MINUTES • COOKING TIME 15 MINUTES (plus standing time)

2 cups (400g) jasmine rice
3¹/₂ cups (875ml) water

1 Rinse rice in strainer under cold water until water is clear.

2 Combine water and rice in heavy-base pan, bring to boil, stirring, reduce heat, simmer gently, covered with a tight fitting lid, 12 minutes. Remove from heat, stand, covered, 10 minutes. It is important not to remove lid during cooking and steaming.

3 Fluff rice with fork.

SERVES 4

store Can be made a day ahead. Store, covered, in refrigerator. Suitable to freeze.

per serving 0.5g fat; 1470kJ

Combining rice and water

Fluffing rice with a fork

noodles with prawns and green capsicum

PREPARATION TIME 15 MINUTES • COOKING TIME 10 MINUTES

1 tablespoon oil
2 cloves garlic, crushed
1 large fresh red chilli, sliced
1 medium green capsicum (200g), sliced
2 green onions, chopped
2 tablespoons oyster sauce
1 tablespoon fish sauce
2 teaspoons sugar
2 teaspoons cornflour
1 cup (250ml) chicken stock
250g small cooked prawns, shelled
500g fresh rice noodles

Stir-frying chilli, capsicum and onion

1 Heat oil in wok, stir-fry garlic, chilli, capsicum and onion for 1 minute; remove from wok.

2 Combine sauces and sugar in wok. Blend cornflour with stock, add mixture to wok. Stir over heat until mixture boils and thickens.

3 Return vegetables to wok with prawns and noodles, stir-fry until hot.

SERVES 6

store Best made close to serving.
per serving 3.8g fat; 655kJ

Stir-frying until hot

spicy fried rice

PREPARATION TIME 30 MINUTES (plus standing time) • COOKING TIME 30 MINUTES

1 cup (200g) long grain rice
1/2 cup (10g) dried
**   shiitake mushrooms**
400g can baby corn, drained
500g cooked king prawns,
**   shelled**
1/4 cup (60ml) oil
3 eggs, lightly beaten
1 medium brown onion
**   (150g), chopped**
2 cloves garlic, crushed
1 pork butterfly steak (160g),
**   chopped**
2 seafood sticks (70g), sliced
1 medium green capsicum
**   (200g), chopped**
1 tablespoon curry paste
2 tablespoons light soy sauce
1 tablespoon fish sauce
1 tablespoon chopped fresh
**   coriander leaves**

1 Rinse rice under cold water, drain. Add rice to large pan of boiling water. Boil, uncovered, for about 10 minutes or until tender, drain, rinse rice under cold water; drain well.

2 Place mushrooms in bowl, cover with warm water, stand 20 minutes. Drain mushrooms, discard stems, cut caps into thin slices. Cut corn into quarters. Cut prawns in half lengthways.

3 Heat 1 tablespoon of the oil in wok, add eggs; stir uncooked egg to outside edge of wok, cook until firm. Remove omelette from wok, roll up firmly, cut into thin slices.

4 Heat remaining oil in wok, stir-fry onion and garlic 30 seconds. Add pork, stir-fry until browned. Add prawns, seafood sticks, capsicum and paste, stir-fry 2 minutes. Add rice, sauces and coriander, stir-fry until hot. Serve rice topped with omelette slices.

SERVES 6

store Rice can be prepared a day ahead. Store, covered, in refrigerator.
per serving 15.9g fat; 1540kJ

Preparing vegetables

Cooking omelette

Adding coriander

fried rice with chicken

PREPARATION TIME 20 MINUTES • COOKING TIME 25 MINUTES (plus refrigerating time)

2 cups (400g) long grain rice
¼ cup (60ml) oil
1 medium brown onion
** (150g), chopped**
2 cloves garlic, crushed
1 small red capsicum
** (150g), chopped**
1 cup (170g) chopped
** cooked chicken**
2 eggs, lightly beaten
¼ cup (60ml) fish sauce
1 tablespoon chopped fresh
** coriander leaves**
3 green onions, chopped

1 Add rice to large pan of boiling water, boil, uncovered, for about 12 minutes or until just tender, drain. Rinse rice under cold water; drain well. Spread rice over tray, cover, refrigerate overnight.

2 Heat oil in wok, cook brown onion, stirring, until soft. Stir in garlic and capsicum, stir-fry until capsicum is soft. Add rice and chicken, stir-fry until hot.

3 Stir in eggs quickly, stir-fry until cooked; stir in sauce. Serve, sprinkled with coriander and green onion.

SERVES 4

store Best made close to serving. Rice best prepared a day ahead. Store, covered, in refrigerator.
per serving 21g fat; 2610kJ

Adding cooked rice to pan

Stirring in fish sauce

Poaching squid separately

Stirring in vinegar mixture

seafood, pork and chicken noodles

PREPARATION TIME 40 MINUTES • COOKING TIME 20 MINUTES

**1 teaspoon chopped fresh
    coriander root**
**1/2 teaspoon cracked
    black peppercorns**
4 cloves garlic, crushed
**3 medium fresh red chillies,
    chopped**
2 tablespoons light soy sauce
2 tablespoons white vinegar
2 tablespoons lime juice
1 1/2 tablespoons sugar
300g uncooked prawns
100g squid hoods
150g pork fillet
200g chicken breast fillet
150g rice vermicelli
**1 small red capsicum
    (150g), sliced**
3 green onions, chopped
1/4 cup fresh coriander leaves
3 hard-boiled eggs, quartered

1 Grind coriander root, peppercorns, garlic and chillies into a paste using mortar and pestle. Place paste in jar with sauce, vinegar, juice and sugar; shake well.

2 Shell prawns, leaving tails intact. Cut squid into 2cm square pieces, score inside surface with a sharp knife. Poach prawns, squid, pork and chicken separately in a pan of simmering water until tender; drain, cut chicken and pork into pieces.

3 Cook vermicelli in a pan of boiling water for about 3 minutes or until tender; drain.

4 Cut vermicelli into shorter lengths with scissors. Combine vermicelli in bowl with pork, chicken, seafood, capsicum, onion and coriander. Stir in vinegar mixture. Serve warm or cold, topped with egg.

SERVES 6

store Noodles can be cooked a day ahead. Store, covered, in refrigerator.
per serving 5.4g fat; 998kJ

fried noodles with garlic pork

PREPARATION TIME 15 MINUTES • COOKING TIME 15 MINUTES

175g dried egg noodles
2 tablespoons oil
2 cloves garlic, crushed
250g pork fillet, chopped
1/2 cup (75g) chopped peanuts
1/4 cup (30g) dried shrimp
6 green onions, chopped
2 tablespoons fish sauce
1 teaspoon palm sugar
1 small fresh red chilli,
**   finely chopped**
2 tablespoons lime juice
2 tablespoons chopped fresh
**   coriander leaves**

1 Add noodles to large pan of boiling water, boil, uncovered, for about 5 minutes or until tender; drain well.

2 Heat oil in wok, stir-fry garlic and pork until pork is browned.

3 Add peanuts, shrimp, onion, sauce, sugar, chilli and juice, stir-fry 1 minute.

4 Stir in noodles and coriander, stir-fry until hot.

SERVES 4

store Best made just before serving.
per serving 20.3g fat; 1854kJ

Adding noodles to boiling water

Adding peanuts to pan

Stir-frying until hot

sweet puffed noodles

PREPARATION TIME 15 MINUTES • COOKING TIME 10 MINUTES

100g rice vermicelli
oil for deep-frying
3 teaspoons oil, extra
2 cloves garlic, crushed
100g minced chicken
1 egg, lightly beaten
¹/₄ cup (55g) sugar
2 tablespoons water
1 tablespoon white vinegar
300g small cooked prawns,
    shelled
2 green onions, chopped

1 Deep-fry vermicelli in hot oil in batches until puffed; drain on absorbent paper.

2 Heat 2 teaspoons of the extra oil in small pan, cook garlic, stirring, 1 minute. Add chicken, cook, stirring, further minute or until cooked; remove from pan.

3 Heat remaining extra oil in pan, add egg, swirl to coat base of pan. Cook omelette 1 minute each side, remove. Roll firmly, cut into 5mm slices.

4 Combine sugar, water and vinegar in small pan, stir over heat until sugar is dissolved. Combine noodles, chicken mixture, prawns, onion, omelette strips and sugar syrup in large bowl, toss lightly.

SERVES 6

store Best made just before serving.
per serving 9g fat; 831.6kJ

Deep-frying vermicelli

Cutting omelette into slices

Adding sugar syrup to salad

desserts

Desserts are not usually served after a Thai meal but often appear at banquets and festive occasions; a wide variety of delightful sweets are also sold by street vendors. You'll find that our recipes are delicious at any time – either as after-dinner desserts or in-between snacks.

coconut bananas with caramel sauce

PREPARATION TIME 10 MINUTES • COOKING TIME 15 MINUTES

4 medium firm bananas (800g)
plain flour
2 eggs, beaten lightly
1 cup (70g) shredded coconut
2 tablespoons packaged
   breadcrumbs
oil for deep-frying

CARAMEL SAUCE
1/2 cup (100g) brown sugar,
   firmly packed
1/2 cup (110g) caster sugar
1/2 cup (125ml) water
340g can coconut milk
1 tablespoon arrowroot
1 tablespoon water, extra
20g butter

1 Cut bananas in half lengthways, toss in flour, shake away excess flour. Dip bananas in eggs, then in combined coconut and breadcrumbs.

2 Deep-fry bananas in hot oil until lightly browned; drain on absorbent paper. Serve hot, with caramel sauce.

caramel sauce Combine sugars and water in pan, stir over heat, without boiling, until sugars are dissolved. Bring to boil. Boil, uncovered, for about 8 minutes, or until golden brown. Stir in coconut milk and blended arrowroot and extra water. Stir until sauce thickens slightly, remove from heat, add butter, stir until melted.

SERVES 4

storage Sauce can be made 3 hours ahead. Store sauce, covered, in refrigerator.
per serving 65.3g fat; 4238kJ

Deep-frying bananas

Preparing caramel sauce

sticky rice custard

PREPARATION TIME 15 MINUTES • COOKING TIME 1¹/₂ HOURS (plus cooling and refrigeration time)

¹/₂ cup (100g) short grain rice
2 tablespoons brown sugar
1 cup (250ml) coconut milk
1 cup (250ml) water
1 teaspoon white sesame seeds, toasted

CUSTARD
4 eggs
1 cup (250ml) coconut milk
2 tablespoons sugar

1 Lightly grease 6 (¹/₂ cup capacity) ovenproof dishes. Combine rice, sugar, coconut milk and water in pan, stir over heat until sugar is dissolved. Bring to boil; simmer, uncovered, stirring occasionally, for about 20 minutes, or until nearly all the liquid has been absorbed.

2 Spread rice evenly into prepared dishes. Pour custard evenly over rice. Sprinkle with seeds.

3 Place dishes in baking dish, pour in enough hot water to come halfway up sides of dishes; cover dishes with foil. Bake in moderate oven for about 1 hour until custard is set. Remove dishes from water, cool, refrigerate until cold. Serve custards with fresh fruit, if desired.

custard Whisk eggs, milk and sugar together in bowl.

MAKES 6

store Can be made 2 days ahead. Store, covered, in refrigerator.
per serving 24.1g fat; 1452kJ

Adding hot water to baking dish

Whisking together custard

Adding sugar to bowl

Folding cream into mango mixture

mango ice-cream

PREPARATION TIME 20 MINUTES (plus freezing time) • COOKING TIME 5 MINUTES

You will need 4 ripe mangoes for this recipe.

1 tablespoon gelatine
1/4 cup (60ml) water
3 cups (600g) chopped mango
3/4 cup (165g) caster sugar
1 tablespoon orange juice
300ml thickened cream

1 Soften gelatine in water in cup; stir over simmering water until dissolved.

2 Pour gelatine mixture into bowl, stir in mango, sugar and orange juice; stir until sugar is dissolved. Place mixture in lamington pan; cover, freeze for about 1 hour or until firm, process until pale in colour.

3 Whip cream until soft peaks form; fold into mango mixture. Return to lamington pan; cover, freeze several hours or overnight. Remove from freezer 15 minutes before serving.

SERVES 4

store Can be made a week ahead. Store, covered, in freezer.
per serving 27.9g fat; 2159kJ

coconut rose custard

PREPARATION TIME 15 MINUTES
COOKING TIME 25 MINUTES (plus cooling time)

1²/₃ cups (410ml) coconut cream
5 eggs, lightly beaten
¹/₂ cup (100g) brown sugar, firmly packed
1 tablespoon rose water
2 tablespoons coconut

1 Combine all ingredients in pan; stir over heat until warm; do not boil.

2 Pour mixture into greased 22cm shallow round ovenproof dish. Place dish in baking dish, pour in enough boiling water to come halfway up side of dish.

3 Bake in moderate oven for about 20 minutes or until centre of custard is just set. Remove custard from baking dish, cool. Refrigerate custard before serving. Cut into wedges and sprinkle with extra coconut, if desired.

SERVES 4

store Can be made a day ahead. Store, covered, in refrigerator.
per serving 19.7g fat; 1149kJ

Adding coconut

Pouring boiling water into baking dish

sweet potato and cardamom ice-cream

PREPARATION TIME 20 MINUTES (plus freezing time) • COOKING TIME 20 MINUTES (plus cooling time)

350g kumara, finely chopped
2 cups (500ml) milk
¹/₄ cup (55g) sugar
1¹/₂ teaspoons ground cardamom
400g can sweetened
  condensed milk
300ml thickened cream

1 Combine kumara, milk, sugar and cardamom in pan; stir without boiling until sugar is dissolved. Bring to boil, simmer, covered, for about 15 minutes or until kumara is tender; cool.

2 Blend or process kumara mixture in batches until smooth. Blend in condensed milk. Pour into lamington pan; cover, freeze several hours or until partially set.

3 Beat kumara mixture with cream in large bowl with electric mixer or process until combined. Return to lamington pan; cover, freeze overnight. Serve sprinkled with nuts, if desired.

SERVES 6

store Can be made a week ahead. Store, covered, in freezer.
per serving 28g fat; 2186kJ

Adding condensed milk

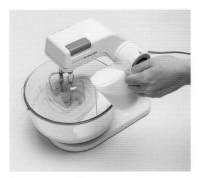

Adding cream to kumara mixture

Adding lime juice to syrup

Pouring sugar syrup over salad

tropical fruits in lime syrup

PREPARATION TIME 15 MINUTES • COOKING TIME 25 MINUTES (plus cooling time)

2 cups (440g) sugar
2 cups (500ml) water
¹/₄ cup (60ml) lime juice
¹/₂ rockmelon (1.3kg), sliced
¹/₂ honeydew melon
 (750g), sliced
1 small papaw (650g), sliced
1 small pineapple (800g), sliced
375g lychees, seeded

1 Combine sugar, water and lime juice in pan, stir over heat without boiling until sugar is dissolved. Bring to the boil, boil rapidly, uncovered, without stirring for about 20 minutes or until syrup is thick; cool, refrigerate.

2 Pour syrup over fruit; mix gently.

SERVES 4

store Can be prepared 2 days ahead. Store, covered, in refrigerator.
per serving 1.3g fat; 2854kJ

lychee, ginger and lime ice

PREPARATION TIME 15 MINUTES (plus freezing time)
COOKING TIME 10 MINUTES (plus cooling time)

425g can lychees
2^1/$_2$ cups (625ml) water
1^1/$_2$ cups (330g) caster sugar
1 teaspoon grated fresh ginger
1 large orange (300g), segmented
1 teaspoon grated lime rind
^{1}/$_4$ cup (60ml) lime juice

1 Drain lychees, reserve syrup. Combine water, sugar and reserved syrup in pan, stir over heat, without boiling, until sugar is dissolved. Bring to boil, stir in ginger, continue boiling, uncovered, 5 minutes.

2 Chop orange segments. Stir into lychee syrup with rind and juice, simmer, uncovered, 3 minutes; cool.

3 Pour mixture into lamington pan, cover, freeze for about 2 hours or until almost firm. Transfer mixture to bowl, beat with fork. Return to tray, cover, freeze until firm. Serve ice with lychees.

SERVES 6

store Ice can be made 3 days ahead. Store ice, covered, in freezer. Store lychees, covered, in refrigerator.
per serving 0.1g fat; 1138kJ

Adding ginger to boiling syrup

Pouring mixture into lamington pan

glossary

SAMBAL OELEK

SMALL BIRDSEYE CHILLIES

LARGE FRESH CHILLIES

DRIED CHILLI FLAKES

DRIED CHILLIES

CHILLI POWDER

bamboo shoots the tender shoots of bamboo plants, available in cans.

bamboo skewers can be used instead of metal skewers if soaked in water overnight or for several hours to prevent burning during cooking. They are available in several lengths.

bamboo steamer available in various sizes, the base should be soaked in cold water for 10 minutes before using.

beef

EYE FILLET tender-loin.

MINCED BEEF ground beef.

blend or process to "blend or process" ingredients means that a good result will be obtained by either blending or processing. However, "blend" alone means a food processor won't do the job finely enough.

bok choy also called pak choi or Chinese white cabbage; has a fresh, mild mustard taste.

breadcrumbs

PACKAGED DRY fine-textured, crunchy, purchased white breadcrumbs.

STALE use 1- or 2-day-old white bread made into crumbs by grating, blending or processing.

calamari also known as squid.

cardamom an expensive spice with an exotic fragrance. It can be bought in pod, seed or ground form.

BOK CHOY AND BABY BOK CHOY

chicken

BREAST FILLETS skinless, boneless fillets cut from the breast available whole or in halves.

THIGH FILLETS skinless, boneless fillets cut from the thigh.

chillies available in many different types, both fresh and dried. Use rubber gloves when seeding and chopping fresh chillies as they can burn your skin. Removing seeds and membranes lessens the heat level.

chinese cabbage also known as Peking cabbage or Napa cabbage; resembles a cos lettuce but tastes similar to the common round cabbage.

cinnamon fragrant bark used as a spice; available in sticks (quills) or ground.

cloves dried flower buds of a tropical tree; available whole or ground.

coconut use desiccated coconut unless otherwise specified. To toast, stir coconut in pan over heat until lightly browned, remove from pan, cool.

CREAM available in cans; coconut milk can be substituted, although it is not as thick.

FLAKED coconut flesh flaked and dried.

MILK can be bought in cans but is easy to make using desiccated coconut. (See "Thai Essential Ingredients" on pages 4-5.) Note: coconut milk is not the liquid inside the mature coconut.

POWDERED

MILK a substitute for coconut milk, but is not as rich as coconut cream.

SHREDDED coconut flesh shredded and dried.

cornflour also known as cornstarch; used as a thickening agent in cooking.

cumin available in seeds or ground.

curry paste prepared paste available in jars in supermarkets, delicatessens and specialty food shops.

curry powder a convenient combination of spices in powdered form. Curry powder consists of chilli, coriander, cumin, fennel, fenugreek and turmeric in varying proportions.

five-spice powder a fragrant mixture of ground cinnamon, cloves, fennel seeds, star anise and Sichuan peppers.

galangal the dried root of a plant of the ginger family. It is used as a flavouring, and is either removed before serving or left uneaten.

FRESH AND DRIED GALANGAL

ginger

FRESH, GREEN OR ROOT GINGER the thick, gnarled root of a tropical plant; scrape away outside skin and grate, chop or slice ginger, as required. Fresh, peeled ginger can be preserved by covering with dry sherry and storing in refrigerator; it will keep for several months. It can also be frozen in an airtight container.

GROUND is also available but is not a substitute for fresh ginger.

gow gee wrappers wonton wrappers, spring rolls or egg pastry sheets can be substituted in cooking.

herbs we have specified when to use fresh or dried herbs. We used dried (not ground) herbs in the proportion of 1:4 for fresh herbs. For example, use 1 teaspoon dried herbs instead of 4 teaspoons (1 tablespoon) chopped fresh herbs.

hoisin sauce a thick, sweet and spicy Chinese paste made from salted fermented soy beans, onions and garlic; used as a marinade or baste, or to accent stir-fries and barbecued or roasted foods.

kumara Polynesian name of orange-fleshed sweet potato, often confused with yam.

lamb

FILLET a small tender cut found between the loin and chump.

manjo mirin a sweet rice wine vinegar used for cooking.

mortar and pestle Thais use clay mortars with wooden pestles specially made to cope with small amounts of moist curry pastes and for bruising lemon grass, citrus rind, garlic and coriander root.

mushrooms
BABY cultivated mushrooms.
DRIED SHIITAKE unique in flavour; soak in hot water, covered, for 20 minutes, drain. Remove and discard stems, use caps as indicated in recipes.
STRAW available in cans.

noodles
FRESH EGG made from wheat flour and eggs, sold in strands of varying thickness.
FRESH RICE thick, wide, almost white in colour; made from rice and vegetable oil. Must be covered with boiling water to remove starch and excess oil before using in soups and stir-fries.
HOKKIEN also known as stir-fry noodles; fresh wheat flour noodles resembling thick, yellow-brown spaghetti needing no pre-cooking before use.
RICE VERMICELLI also known as rice flour noodles; made from ground rice, dried and best used either deep-fried or soaked, then tossed in a stir-fry or stirred into a soup.

oil use a good-quality vegetable or peanut oil unless otherwise specified.

onion
GREEN also known as scallion or (incorrectly) shallot; an immature onion picked before the bulb has formed, having a long, bright green, edible stalk.
RED also known as Spanish, red Spanish or Bermuda onion; a sweet-flavoured, large, purple-red onion that is particularly good eaten raw in salads.
SPRING has a crisp, narrow, green leafed top and a fairly large sweet white bulb.

oyster sauce a rich brown sauce made from oysters and their brine, cooked with salt and soy sauce, then thickened with starches.

pawpaw also known as papaya.

peanuts we used the roasted unsalted variety.

pork
BUTTERFLY STEAK skinless, boneless mid-loin chop which has been split in half and opened out flat.
FILLETS skinless, boneless eye-fillet from the loin.

prawns also known as shrimp.

rice There are several ways to cook rice. One method is add the rice gradually to a pan of boiling water, boil rapidly, uncovered, for about 10 minutes or until rice is just tender; drain and serve immediately.

The other method, the absorption method, is easy and traditional in Asian countries.

Rice can also be cooked in a rice cooker. Follow the manufacturer's instructions, or use the absorption method. To reheat rice, place covered in a strainer over boiling water, or reheat in a microwave oven.

Cold, cooked rice can be frozen in airtight bags or containers for several months.
FLOUR ground rice.
GLUTINOUS (sweet or sticky rice) when cooked has a soft chewy texture.
JASMINE Thai long grain rice.
LONG GRAIN elongated grains.
SHORT GRAIN about half the length of long grain rice, but thicker.

rind zest.

rockmelon also known as cantaloupe.

rose water an extract made from crushed rose petals.

saffron this is the most expensive of all spices. Available in threads or ground form; it impart a yellow-orange colour to food; it remains fresh longer if refrigerated.

sambal oelek originally from Indonesia, a salty paste made from ground chillies vinegar and spices.

seafood sticks made from processed Alaskan pollack flavoured with crab.

sesame oil made from roasted, crushed white sesame seeds. Use in small quantities for flavour. Do not use for frying.

sesame seeds there are two main types: black and white, though there are also red and brown varieties; we use white sesame seeds in this book.

snow peas also known as mange tout ("eat all").

soy sauce made from fermented soy beans. Several varieties are available in supermarkets and Asian food stores.

spring roll wrappers see gow gee wrappers.

sprouts
BEAN also known as bean shoots; tender new growths of assorted beans and seeds germinated for consumption as sprouts. The most readily available are mung bean, soy bean, alfalfa and snow pea sprouts. We used mung bean shoots in this book.

squid a type of mollusc, sometimes known as calamari. Cleaned squid hoods are available.

sugar we used coarse white granulated, table sugar, also known as crystal sugar, unless otherwise specified.
BROWN soft, fine, brown sugar.
CASTER very, fine white, granulated sugar; also known as superfine sugar.
PALM fine sugar from the coconut palm. It is sold in cakes, also known as gula jawa, gula melaka and jaggery. Palm sugar can be replaced with brown or black sugar.
RAW natural, light brown, granulated sugar or "sugar in the raw".

tamarind sauce a thick, concentrated purple-black, ready to use paste extracted

SNOW PEA SPROUTS

from the pulp of the tamarind bean; use as it is for a tart, sweet-sour taste. If concentrate is unavailable, soak 30g dried tamarind in a cup of hot water, stand 10 minutes, allow to cool, squeeze pulp as dry as possible and use the flavoured water.

tofu also known as bean curd, an off-white custard-like product made from boiled, crushed soy beans. There are two main types: cotton tofu and silken tofu, which is more soft and fragile. Store, covered with water, in the refrigerator and change water daily. We used cotton tofu in this book.

turmeric a member of the ginger family, its root is ground and dried, yielding the yellow powder that gives curry its colour. It is not hot in flavour.

vinegar we used both white and brown (malt) vinegar in this book.
RICE seasoned vinegar containing sugar and salt.

white fish fillets we used flake unless otherwise specified. Any white fish can be used.

wine we used good-quality red and white wines.

zucchini also known as courgette.

PALM SUGAR

conversion chart

MEASURES

One Australian metric measuring cup holds approximately 250ml; one Australian metric tablespoon holds 20ml; one Australian metric teaspoon holds 5ml.

The difference between one country's measuring cups and another's is within a two- or three-teaspoon variance, and will not affect your cooking results. North America, New Zealand and the United Kingdom use a 15ml tablespoon.

All cup and spoon measurements are level. The most accurate way of measuring dry ingredients is to weigh them. When measuring liquids, use a clear glass or plastic jug with the metric markings. We use large eggs with an average weight of 60g.

DRY MEASURES

METRIC	IMPERIAL
15g	½oz
30g	1oz
60g	2oz
90g	3oz
125g	4oz (¼lb)
155g	5oz
185g	6oz
220g	7oz
250g	8oz (½lb)
280g	9oz
315g	10oz
345g	11oz
375g	12oz (¾lb)
410g	13oz
440g	14oz
470g	15oz
500g	16oz (1lb)
750g	24oz (1½lb)
1kg	32oz (2lb)

LIQUID MEASURES

METRIC	IMPERIAL
30ml	1 fluid oz
60ml	2 fluid oz
100ml	3 fluid oz
125ml	4 fluid oz
150ml	5 fluid oz (¼ pint/1 gill)
190ml	6 fluid oz
250ml	8 fluid oz
300ml	10 fluid oz (½ pint)
500ml	16 fluid oz
600ml	20 fluid oz (1 pint)
1000ml (1 litre)	1¾ pints

LENGTH MEASURES

METRIC	IMPERIAL
3mm	⅛in
6mm	¼in
1cm	½in
2cm	¾in
2.5cm	1in
5cm	2in
6cm	2½in
8cm	3in
10cm	4in
13cm	5in
15cm	6in
18cm	7in
20cm	8in
23cm	9in
25cm	10in
28cm	11in
30cm	12in (1ft)

OVEN TEMPERATURES

These oven temperatures are only a guide for conventional ovens. For fan-forced ovens, check the manufacturer's manual.

	°C (CELSIUS)	°F (FAHRENHEIT)	GAS MARK
Very slow	120	250	½
Slow	150	275-300	1-2
Moderately slow	160	325	3
Moderate	180	350-375	4-5
Moderately hot	200	400	6
Hot	220	425-450	7-8
Very hot	240	475	9

index

This edition published in 2012 by Octopus Publishing Group Limited
based on materials licensed to it by ACP Magazines Ltd,
a division of PBL Media Pty Limited
54 Park St, Sydney
GPO Box 4088, Sydney, NSW 2001.
phone (02) 9282 8618; fax (02) 9267 9438
acpbooks@acpmagazines.com.au; www.acpbooks.com.au

ACP BOOKS
General Manager - Christine Whiston
Editor-in-Chief - Susan Tomnay
Creative Director - Hieu Chi Nguyen
Food Director - Pamela Clark

OCTOPUS BOOKS
Published and Distributed in the United Kingdom by
Octopus Publishing Group Limited
Endeavour House
189 Shaftesbury Avenue
London WC2H 8JY
United Kingdom
phone (+44)(0)207 632 5400; fax (+44)(0)207 632 5405
aww@octopusbooks.co.uk; www.octopusbooks.co.uk;
www.australian-womens-weekly.com

Printed and bound in China

International foreign language rights, Brian Cearnes, ACP Books bcearnes@acpmagazines.com.au

A catalogue record for this book is available from the British Library.
ISBN 978-1-907428-63-0
© ACP Magazines Ltd 2010
ABN 18 053 273 546

This book was originally published in 1991. Reprinted 1991, 1992, 1994, 1995, 1996,
1997, 1998 (twice), 2000, 2001, 2002, 2003, 2004, 2007, 2008, 2009 and 2010.

To order Australian Women's Weekly Books:
telephone LBS on 01903 828 503
or order online at www.australian-womens-weekly.com
or www.octopusbooks.co.uk